Black

Princess

A Guide For Young Females...

Written and edited by:
David H. Horton, II

Copyright © 2009
By
David H. Horton, II
Owner Author Extraordinaire
Negro Publishing, LLC

Library of Congress Control Number: 2009905298

ISBN: 978-0-9763583-1-2

Printed in the United States by
Morris Publishing
3212 East Highway 30
Kearney, NE 68847
1-800-650-7888

Another book by Negro Publishing, LLC

www.negropublishing.com

<u>Black Princess - A Guide For Young Females</u>

This is book is dedicated to the following young ladies:

- My sisters: Ms. Danita Horton, Ms. Latima Horton, Ms. Fatima Horton, and Ms. Crystal Sanders.
- Ms. Jasmine Horton
- Ms. Shaniece Ra'Gine Perry
- Ms. Sanaa Perry
- Ms. Autumn Alston
- Ms. Mckenzie Kiel
- Ms. Jayla Burwell
- Ms. Kennedy Burwell
- Ms. Ava Cash
- Ms. Rachel Odister
- Ms. Alison Elle Chambers
- Ms. Sarai Alina Davis
- Ms. Bria Donnell
- Ms. Kristian Bryant
- Ms. Havana Farinas
- Ms. Gabriella R. Williams
- Ms. Saraah and Ms. Rebekah Cardwell
- Ms. Sejal Bowens
- Ms. Taylor Wade Downey
- Ms. A'lise Holliday
- Ms. Jillian Camille Smith
- Ms. Kabirah Wellons

Foreword:

Hello everyone,

When my son David (Supa Dave to his crew) first asked me to write the foreword to this book I was elated.   Early on when he shared with me that his next book would be for young women, my immediate thoughts were that he didn't know anything about women - and that dating a hundred or so women does not make you an expert on them (*Editor's Note: MOM!!!*).   However, David has always been diligent in his efforts and when he sets his mind to something he aims to do a good job.

David has always been interested in writing and was an avid reader by the age of six years old.   By the time he was eight years old, he would proof-read documents for me after we finished his spelling homework.

My child is an adventurer.   He likes to experience new things.   We have had numerous battles over the years but I now realize he was just practicing political discussions.   Not only have I found out that he was paying attention to me but he also learned something.   Wow!

After reading selected titles, I see that he does have a general understanding of women.   He realizes that we are different and need help understanding men.   He's not just re-hashing the same old relationship advice – he is concerned with the totality of the young female.

In the book, he relates to women on a friendly level that lets you feel as if you are truly having a conversation with him.   David covers topics the way he feels we should look at them.

I was especially impressed with the subject matter dedicated to tattoos.   It is here that I noted that he doesn't share what his tattoos were because he is more intent on the young female putting thought into her personal choice of tattoo.   I'm personally against tattoos but was proud of the thought that he put into his own.   For the record, his first tattoo was praying hands which to me says "prayer first", something I've worked hard on instilling in him since he was a young child who wanted to watch church on TV.

Dave covers a range of topics including men's inability to verbally communicate versus their usage of sign language or as he puts it "man-speak" to convey their desires. My young man does an outstanding job of writing about heart, soul, health, and food with humor and history. David also demonstrates a tremendous amount of sensitivity with personal issues including dating, friendship, and crazy actions. He even managed to take a humorous shot at my cooking skills.

This book will provide a road map for many young ladies wondering about what life brings. It will enlighten young ladies as to how males think including what they believe about women. It was once said that if one person writes a letter then thousands of other people feel the same way and just didn't write.

So please take my invitation to enjoy my son's work. As you listen to the concepts I hope you can appreciate a young man sharing his viewpoint. God bless and thank you for reading.

Dr. Jenny Perry Horton
Educator, Mother, and Friend

Table of Contents

CHAPTER 1.

Tupac's call to action

"Some say the blacker the berry, the sweeter the juice

I say the darker the flesh then the deeper the roots

I give a holler to my sisters on welfare

Tupac cares,

if don't nobody else care

And uhh, I know they like to beat ya down a lot

When you come around the block brothas clown a lot

But please don't cry, dry your eyes, never let up

Forgive but don't forget,

girl keep your head up

And when he tells you that you ain't nuttin don't believe him

And if he can't learn to love you

then you should leave him

Cause sista you don't need him

And I ain't tryin to gas ya up,

I just call em how I see 'em

Black Princess - A Guide For Young Females

You know what makes me unhappy (what's that?)

When brothas make babies, and leave a young mother to be a pappy

And since we all came from a woman

Got our name from a woman and our game from a woman

I wonder why we take from our women

Why we rape our women,

do we hate our women?

I think it's time to kill for our women

Time to heal our women,

be REAL to our women

And if we don't - we'll have a race of babies

That will hate the ladies that make the babies

And since a man can't make one

He has no right to tell a woman when and where to create one

So will the real men get up

I know you're fed up ladies,

But keep your head up."

"Keep ya head up"
-Tupac Shakur

(Excerpt from the song "Keep ya Head up" reprinted with permission pending through Universal Music Publishing)

CHAPTER 2.

BACK AGAIN...

What up?   It's me! Back again, and I'm here to do something that has never been done before.   But hey, that's just me – that's what I do.   But penning a guide for young females? By a young male? Hmmmm... Who does this guy think he is?   Who?   Well, I'm me. David H. Horton, II and I'm just the guy for the job.

I've put a lot of time, energy and relations into this book hoping to craft something worthwhile and memorable.   This isn't something just whipped up with some celebrity endorsements.   This is from me to all the young ladies out there so I hope you enjoy it.

The task that I have decided to take upon myself is one that has led me down many mysterious path ways.   Yes, I have decided to tell women what to do - sorta.   Craziness right?   Or is it?   When was the last time the black female REALLY heard from the black male about how we see things?   Magazines don't count either – they'll tell you to play 'hard to get' while putting out a magazine with nothing but half-naked women in it.   Trust me – guys only look at the pictures anyway.

There have been other attempts to do what I'm doing but I'm not sure some of those attempts were in the best interests of you females. Rarely are they well-rounded.   You've been given a lot of dessert but no real meat.   I plan on giving you more than just a little to get by and make you ask more questions.

What's really amazing is that this book has been hard for me.   I cried several times writing this book.   Putting my heart into this meant more than marketing or sales.

All my life I've always been able to pretty much do what I wanted to do simply off natural talent.   Writing is one of the few things that allows me to go deep within myself and find out what truly challenges and interests me. But a book for females? Geez!

Writing a book for females has conjured up a number of feelings. Which way do I go? How do I offer advice? Will I be too harsh? Will I have every Black Woman in America hating my guts? Is it possible to be a father figure, a brother, and a friend without being hypocritical? Or even worse – judgmental?

Even this intro was hard for me to write because I understand that it sets the tone for the entire book. With my first book, 'Negro Intellect', my audience was me, my friends and those that I knew would benefit from sound advice and a few tricks of the trade. This book however is a whole other animal.

So how does a man, a 'regular joe' so to speak, tell black women what they need to do? Delicately I assume - and with caution, because I don't want to incur the wrath of Oprah. But then again, that would be idiocy. I'm never scared. Oprah should call ME up and ask for advice. There are just certain things going on with women that need to be addressed. Class has been replaced with glitz. Home cooked meals have been replaced with salaries and take out meals.

Wow! It's serious. I might get hurt because in order to get to the heart of the matter I just may have to hurt some feelings. While I have no problems with that – that is truly not my intention. I simply would like young ladies to behave as such.

I figured something out though and that's the fact that I couldn't write for the ladies without feeling some emotion. I honestly had to get emotional to write this. Writing this I realized how important women are in all of our lives. There aren't many things that make a man emotional but I'll bet the house that the number one thing is a woman.

So how did I become emotional? I did what any man would do – I played Playstation. Football to be exact and it's that manly competitive spirit that allows other feelings to come out.

It is emotion in the heat of the moment. It is purposeful and displayed for better or worse.   Otherwise, I'm not really sure how to turn the emotions on or off which is what scared me about writing a book for females – a group of people that tend to always have their emotions ON.

The fact that my emotions were involved made me realize just how thorough I have to be. I don't want to speak out of spite, confusion, or in a nature where I might sound as if the words aren't out of love. Women deal in that word all of the time but as a Black man it is one that I have had a hard time attaching things too – but I do KNOW what I love.

Love.   That's what this is about.   It's what men need from women. It's what women need from men.   It's what humans need to survive.

YOU should DEMAND love.   But like anything else with poor communication - there's a gap between the black male and female. Hopefully I can help fill in some of the empty spaces as we continue to grow into ourselves as a people and as a family.

It is my opinion that women are the keepers of the flame - the doors to the next generation.   Women have been entrusted by God to be more responsible than man.   Why?   You guys do something we cannot and that is give life. It seems some of the responsibility has been forgotten and intend to shed some light on a few matters.

Black women are confronted with a multitude of issues daily.   I will not even try and sit here and act like I know what it's like to be a black woman.   However, I am a black man and I have a black mother and black sisters.   I deal with black women everyday.   I AM affected by the lives black women lead and therefore, I'd like to holla at yall for a minute.

I AM a big brother and I have younger sisters: Danita, Latima, Fatima and Crystal – who are my angels.   As a big brother my baby sisters are one of my top priorities.   I shall continue to work to insure they have the ability to grow up with a strong male presence in their life and thus be able to develop with nothing to fear.

However, it's not like that for everyone. The importance of the black male in the black female's life is one that is often marginalized but I have witnessed with my own eyes the difference in females who have had strong black males in their life and those who have not.

Ok, I'm a man and I might be a bit clueless about some things but the good thing is that I recognize that. So as I delve into the inner world and inner workings of black life, I bring it to you from the perspective of a young black male – with love. And I swear – I'll be gentle...

Young ladies, prepare to walk with me, on the beach if you like, as we talk about life – and how it really goes down.

Let's do this!!!

CHAPTER 3.

Cooking 101...

Ahem, I'm a man and I get hungry. Even with a new healthy diet I still think about food a lot. Guess what I do when I get hungry? I cook ME some food. Like seriously, I get right in that kitchen and knock it out like I'm doing it for a TV show on the Food Network. It's not Chef Garvin but Chef Supa Dave!!!

Can you cook? Do you know your way around a kitchen? Do you need some reason to learn how to cook? Honestly – do you?

To me, cooking is simple so there's nothing more disturbing to me than when a female can't cook. You can't keep eating fast food and ordering out. Seriously, you'll end up looking like Nicole Richie if you don't learn how to work that skillet or have much money.

What are you gonna do if you have to feed your little brother or sister? What about feeding your own future family? Get-togethers and sleepovers require food too. There's almost no event that isn't complimented by food.

Eating out frequently can be very bad for your health and it is also hard on your moolah. Fast food franchises frequently showcase and feature foods that are high in fat and sodium – two things that are very dangerous to the average person's diet (especially black folks).

I highly encourage you to stay away from anything with a drive-thru, slogan, or menu that only has fried food on it. McDonald's and Chik Fil'A are gonna kill us. I hate to say it but I'm tired of seeing fat folks walking out the wing spot!

Now back to cooking, it's easy! Straight up - cooking is a piece of cake. BUT there is something hard about it and it's called "practice". You can't attempt to cook and then expect to be good at it when you want to impress someone.

Never underestimate a prepared meal. Home cooking is good for the soul. You get the satisfaction of preparing your own food and knowing what's in your meal. You also get to eat your food HOT and on a plate for less than a quarter of what restaurants charge.

I'm from a big family that traditionally has always cooked lots of food. However, my mom was like the baby of the family and therefore she's also one of the worst cooks because she did the least amount of cooking growing up. This has never stopped her from cooking. She'll try and cook anything. She experiments for sure and I love her for it. Some of that stuff just be crazy though. Ha!!! (I love you ma!) We have a lot of dishes in America that people love because someone was experimenting and/or practicing. That's how you pay your cooking dues.

If you don't know how to cook – don't be afraid to say so! Take home economics in school to acquire some cooking skills and some basic pointers. My twin sisters are not big fans of high school but they do love going to home economics.

Learn to understand weights and measures. It is very important to understand how to add the right amount of ingredients and spices to your dishes.

Don't be afraid to take a cooking class on your own either. Cooking is an evolution. You can go from scrambled eggs to baked chicken to whole turkeys to "chicken cordon bleu". It can go down in the chef's playground but just remember that no one is born a chef.

You can even become good enough to pursue cooking as a career. There are number of Culinary schools in the country that routinely turn out chefs. There's a lot of people in the country and somebody has GOT to feed them. Hotels, school cafeterias, exhibition centers, restaurants, airports, coliseums, sports arenas, stadiums, and colleges all have large amounts of people that need to be feed. Chefs of very large operations make a LOT of money. Believe dat! You could even get your own TV show.

But let's get back to the food. Come on, who am I kidding right? I might be healthy but every now and then I've got to have me some REAL <u>soul food</u>.   It makes my soul glow. ☺

According to Wikipedia, "**Soul food** is an American cuisine, a selection of foods, and is the traditional cuisine of African Americans of the Southern United States and of black communities beyond. In the mid-1960s, when the Civil Rights Movement was just beginning, "soul" was a common adjective used to describe African American culture, and thus the name "soul food" was derived."

1960? That's what THEY say.   I say it goes back much further than that.   Why? The food traditionally cooked by blacks in the south has always been good for the soul.   It's the food that makes families sit down and appreciate a good life, good friends, and good times.

LONG before the mid-60s, the evening meal was a time for families to get together, and the tradition of communal meals was the perfect environment for conversation and the reciting of oral history and storytelling. Another tradition was the potluck dinner, with each family member bringing a different dish to the dinner.   Potluck dinners are still done to this day and one of the best ways to throw an easy and small party.

Even though I love soul food I have to always remember to do everything in moderation.   It's also a matter of health.   As a cook I always start small and try and eat fresh.   You got to watch how much salt you're putting in your food (cause salt kills..).   It doesn't hurt to count your calories either; it's no need to eat what your body doesn't need.   Watch the grease and cut the cholesterol.   Diabetes and High blood pressure run rampant in the black community so there's no need to tempt fate with over indulgence.

You gotta have food to cook and to get food you have to go grocery shopping! It all begins at the grocery store.   This is where you set the trend for what you will be cooking in your house.   Try and hit the grocery store early in the morning or late at night when it's not that busy.   That way it's well stocked, clean, and free of chaos.   It also helps if you know your way around the grocery store when time is of the essence.

When at the grocery store, buy foods with some specific brands or types in mind.   Keep a grocery list and do your grocery shopping at home before you get to the grocery store.   Get stuff like fruits, vegetables, toiletries, trash bags, beverages. In other words make a list and check the papers for sales before you go to the market.

Oh and don't forget to check the ingredients of the recipes you want to make when you make the shopping list. (Nothing slows down cooks more than some missing ingredients).

Once in the kitchen, begin your preparations.   Make sure things are laid out and that you have the proper utensils and equipment to get the job done.   Go ahead and pre-heat that oven or warm up the grease too − if necessary, and follow the directions accordingly.

Read ALL the directions then get to mixing, sautéing, grilling, chopping, dicing, slicing, boiling, seasoning, tenderizing, marinating, cutting, filleting, browning, basting, and whatever the recipe may require.

Apply heat then watch and wait.   Food could be ready in 5 minutes once you get it down to a science.   Just remember that it takes practice!!!

Hmmmm, I think you're ready.   Let me know what's for dinner too!

CHAPTER 4.

Body by SUPA DAVE...

This is dedicated to all you young ladies out there. Lord knows I can't fathom what you guys go through but one thing I want yall to all know and understand – is that I know it's serious. Your health is not a game.

Your bodies are among the most complex of all those on this earth. Much care and time must go into making sure you not only stay healthy but also stay fit, active and beautiful.

What's that smell? Is that you? Are you that girl? Is your body changing? Man, it's about to be ON in your female life. Goodness gracious! I think about what we have to deal with as young males but young ladies are affected by life on so many different levels.

Man I couldn't imagine having to go through puberty as a woman. Straight up! From what I've heard and seen it is nothing to play with. Ladies let me tell you that I admire your ability to cope with ever changing body conditions and the side effects they bring.

Yes, puberty and all that is stuff that has to be addressed in this book. Now I cant give you much insight on your body changes but I can tell you to consult a doctor whenever you feel the need. One thing I know about women is that yall have no problem going to the doctor and that is to be encouraged because your body is a highly complex temple that should be monitored on a regular basis.

The doctor. Women love going to the doctor. At least that's what it seems like to me. I know that's not really the case but the fact of the matter is that a women has to go and get regular check-ups to insure good health and I encourage you all to find good physicians to attend to you regularly. Be sure to do self breast exams monthly and get a "pap" once a year.

The doctor is oh so important. You've got to help him help you as well. You've got to make sure you do all the self-checks given to you by the doctor. This is especially helpful for females who have a history of breast cancer in their family.

As far as plastic surgery goes, you really shouldn't be worried about it. It definitely shouldn't be considered an option for an alternative to exercise. Results gained through hard work are more cherished and most definitely last longer. Plus, what's wrong with wanting to be healthier? Besides, I'm sure you are way more beautiful than you are giving yourself credit for. Stay uniquely you.

And please, no way I can talk about taking care of your body without mentioning getting tested regularly for STDs and HIV. This testing can save your life and keep you from developing all kinds of sub-diseases that could affect your life and well being. Please – get tested – it will do you nothing but GOOD.

If there's one way to turn a dude off, it's a lack of cleanliness. Some guys don't care but you'd be surprised how many guys want a reasonably clean female. It comes across in so many ways. Cleanliness is not a household chore – it's a lifestyle.

Your hygiene is so important. Your hygiene can set the tone for your entire day. Learning how to take care of your body is one of life's ongoing tasks. You have to make sure you are doing things like brushing your teeth, washing your face, neck, and hair. Please make you take extra special care of all your feminine areas as well.

Natural beauty can be radiant and gourgeous and believe it or not most dudes prefer it. Just avoid the caffeine and wash your face daily. Take care of that skin by wearing sun block when you're out in the sun for extended periods of time. Watch the oily and greasy foods too. Eat fruits and vegetables – they keep many natural vitamins in your system. And please, by all means, drink plenty of water!!!

If you're gonna wear make-up you have to find out what kind of skin you have and what colors look good on you.

There are so many products out there that can help keep you clean and clear. I don't know all of the products for sure but I can tell you what the ladies I know use. Even better, I'll give you the products and some of their websites. Somebody should pay me but really the payment is in you looking your best.

Check out the following folks and their websites:

- M.A.C. Cosmetics is loved by many. www.maccosmetics.com
- Dove, www.dove.us
- Estee Lauder, www.esteelauder.com
- Nivea, www.nivea.com
- Oil of Olay, www.olay.com
- Coco butter, www.etbrowne.com
  (I'm a fan of Palmer's because they have made CoCo Butter much easier to apply now-a-days)
- Carol's daughter, www.CarolsDaughter.com
- Avon, of course, www.avon.com,
- Mary K!, www.marykay.com, home of the Pink Cadillac!
- And lastly, preserve your sexy like Diddy with Pro-Active. www.proactiv.com

And these are just a few. I know that there are MANY more out there. Just send me a sample! ☺

You gotta take care of your entire face as well so don't forget your lips and your mouth. I put Vaseline on my lips before I go to sleep to keep them soft. Don't know if this will work for you but I promise you they wont get chapped! See the dentist at least twice a year to keep the teeth pearly white.

Let's not forget our appendages. Your hands are oh so important to your everyday life so take care of them as well. Make sure you keep them moisturized and your fingernails groomed. There are plenty of places out there that you can get a good manicure but make sure the shop you go to has a good history and a clean bill of health.

While you're taking care of your hands, don't forget your feet.   Your feet are so essential to you living a healthy and productive life.   You can get pedicures for grooming and soak your feet to keep the skin smooth.   You've got to do other things for healthy feet however and one of the most important is wearing the right sized SHOES.   Please don't wear your shoes too small trying to be cute.   You'll regret it – I promise you that.

Moving on...

Tattoos!!!   I know some of you are dying to mark-up your bodies but your mom will not let you.   Guess what? There's an alternative! Not only is it not permanent but it's also safe and you can change it up anytime you want.   It's called the Henna tattoo.

Henna tattoos are an ancient Indian Body Art. They are used in creating intricate ethnic or contemporary designs and exotic patterns on various parts of the body, though traditionally applied to the hands and feet of women preparing for special ceremonies. It is completely natural, non-permanent and painless.

The appeal? They are painless temporary tattoos that are cutting edge, cool, painless, fun, and use NO NEEDLES. It's just a natural paste.

What was in this month might be out the next, so with Henna, a lifetime commitment (like real tattoos) is not necessary as the designs fade within one to four weeks.

We'll get to real tattoos later – it's something a lady has got to put some thought into.

Oh yeah, I almost forgot.   Taking care of your body also requires something called exercise.   You know, you've got to get the blood flowing and clear up some of those blood vessels and arteries.

I'm no expert but they recommend that teens get 60 minutes or more of moderate to vigorous physical activity each day.   I do know that a physically fit person is capable of so much more than those who do nothing at all.

Exercise benefits every part of the body, including the mind. It can even help you look better. Exercise helps people lose weight and lower the risk of some diseases. Exercise can also help a person age well. This may not seem important now, but your body will thank you later.

Exercising to maintain a healthy weight decreases a person's risk of developing certain diseases, including Type 2 diabetes and high blood pressure. These diseases, which used to be found mostly in adults, are becoming more common in teens. Females are especially prone to a condition called osteoporosis (a weakening of the bones) as you get older.

Different types of exercise strengthen different muscle groups, for example: For arms, try rowing or cross-country skiing. Pull-ups and push-ups, those old gym class standbys, are also good for building arm muscles. For strong legs, try running, biking, rowing, or skating. Squats and leg raises also work the legs. For shapely abs, you can't beat rowing, yoga or Pilates, and crunches.

Strengthening the heart and other muscles isn't the only important goal of exercise. Exercise also helps the body stay flexible, meaning that your muscles and joints stretch and bend easily. People who are flexible can worry less about strained muscles and sprains.

One of the biggest reasons people drop an exercise program is lack of interest. If what you're doing isn't fun, it's hard to keep it up. Me? I play basketball almost daily and although I have more sucky days than good ones most of the time, I still love to play the game. Trust me, I'm always waiting on that perfect game and it keeps me feeling like a teenager.

When picking the right type of exercise, it can help to consider your workout personality. For example, do you like to work out alone and on your own schedule? If so, solo sports like biking or running may be for you. Or you could like the shared motivation and companionship that comes from being part of a team. Join an organization or a gym in your area. You'll be able to use those teammates for social interaction and gain knowledge from the group experience.

You also need to plan around practical considerations, such as whether your chosen activity is affordable and available to you. (Activities like horseback riding may be harder for people who live in the hood, for example.) You'll also want to think about how much time you can set aside for your sport.

Another thing to consider is whether any health conditions may affect how — and how much — you exercise. Doctors know that most people benefit from regular exercise, even those with disabilities or conditions like asthma.

If you have a health problem or other considerations (like being overweight, very out of shape, or just plain flabby), talk to your doctor before beginning an exercise plan. That way, you can get information on what exercise programs are best and what to avoid.

Considering the benefits to the heart, muscles, joints, and mind, it's easy to see why exercise is wise. And the great thing about exercise is that it's never too late to start. Even small things can count as exercise when you're starting out — like taking a short bike ride, walking the dog, or raking leaves.

If you're already getting regular exercise now, try to keep it up after you graduate from high school. Staying fit is often one of the biggest challenges for people as they get busy with college and careers.

I think you got it by now. Keeping the body right is a full-time job so please be sure to listen to it when it's talking to you. Besides, you're gonna need all your energy to keep up with folks like me. ☺

CHAPTER 5.

The TRUTH about drugs...

Thanks to medical and drug research, there are thousands of drugs that help people.

Antibiotics and vaccines have revolutionized the treatment of infections. There are medicines to lower blood pressure, treat diabetes, and reduce the body's rejection of new organs.

Medicines can cure, slow, or prevent disease, helping us to lead healthier and happier lives.

However, there are also lots of illegal, harmful drugs that people take to help them feel good or have a good time.

How do drugs work? Drugs are chemicals or substances that change the way our bodies work. When you put them into your body, drugs find their way into your bloodstream and are transported to parts of your body, such as your brain.   Don't know if I need to mention this but ummm, your brain is pretty important for a variety of reasons.

The effects of drugs can vary depending upon the kind of drug taken, how much is taken, how often it is used, how quickly it gets to the brain, and what other drugs, food, or substances are taken at the same time. Effects can also vary based on the differences in body size, shape, and chemistry.

Substances can do a lot of harm to the body and brain. Drinking alcohol, smoking tobacco, taking illegal drugs, and sniffing glue can all cause serious damage to the human body. Some drugs severely impair a person's ability to make healthy choices and decisions.

And just as there are many kinds of drugs available, there are as many reasons for trying drugs or starting to use drugs regularly. People take drugs just for the pleasure they believe they can bring. Often it's because someone tried to convince them that drugs would make them feel good or that they'd have a better time if they took them.

Some teens believe drugs will help them think better, be more popular, stay more active, or become better athletes. Others are simply curious and figure one try won't hurt. Others want to fit in. A few use drugs to gain attention from their parents.

The truth is, drugs don't solve problems. Drugs simply hide feelings and problems. When a drug wears off, the feelings and problems remain - or become worse. Drugs can ruin every aspect of a person's life.

Some of the more common drugs are alcohol, marijuana, cocaine, crack, and crystal meth.

Alcohol is the oldest and most widely used drug in the world, alcohol is a depressant that alters perceptions, emotions, and senses.

Alcohol affects your self-control. Alcohol depresses your central nervous system, lowers your inhibitions, and impairs your judgment. Drinking can lead to risky behaviors, such as driving when you shouldn't, or having unprotected sex.

Alcohol can kill you. Drinking large amounts of alcohol at one time or very rapidly can cause alcohol poisoning, which can lead to coma or even death.

Driving and drinking also can be deadly. In 2003, 31 percent of drivers age 15 to 20 who died in traffic accidents had been drinking alcohol. As a person whose seen a number of his friends die in car accidents, I want you to make the right decision and be responsible.

Alcohol can hurt you--even if you're not the one drinking. If you're around people who are drinking, you have an increased risk of being seriously injured, involved in car crashes, or affected by violence. At the very least, you may have to deal with people who are sick, out of control, or unable to take care of themselves.   Know the law. It is illegal to buy or possess alcohol if you are under age 21.

Get the facts. One drink can make you fail a breath test. In some States, people under age 21 can lose their driver's license, be subject to a heavy fine, or have their car permanently taken away if found guilty of being driving while under the influence of alcohol and/or drugs.

There are drugs like amphetamines which are stimulants that accelerate functions in the brain and body. They are more commonly known as speed.   You should know that you should stay away from anything with a nickname.

Cocaine has destroyed countless lives - directly and indirectly. Cocaine is a white crystalline powder made from the dried leaves of the coca plant. It is commonly known that a form of cocaine was once used in Coca-Cola long ago and it has been used by many people for centuries.   Crack, on the other hand, is newer and more street related.   Crack is named for its crackle when heated and broken up for distribution.

Cocaine is NO joke. First-time users - even teens - of both cocaine and crack can stop breathing or have fatal heart attacks. Using cocaine or crack even one time can kill you.   These drugs are highly addictive, and as a result, the drug, not the user, calls the shots. Even after one use, cocaine and crack can create both physical and psychological cravings that make it very, very difficult for users to stop.   Stay far far away.

Sipping Syrup!!!!   Several over-the-counter cough and cold medicines contain the ingredient dextromethorphan (also called DXM). If taken in large quantities, these over-the-counter medicines can cause hallucinations, loss of motor control, and "out-of-body" sensations.

Small doses help suppress coughing, but larger doses can cause fever, confusion, impaired judgment, blurred vision, dizziness, paranoia, excessive sweating, slurred speech, nausea, vomiting, abdominal pain, irregular heartbeat, high blood pressure, headache, lethargy, numbness of fingers and toes, redness of face, dry and itchy skin, loss of consciousness, seizures, brain damage, and even death.

Yes, death from essentially drinking cough syrup. A number of rapper's deaths can be attributed to complications from mixing the syrupy concoctions along with other ailments and vices.

Ecstasy is also a very popular drug and it is usually taken in a pill form. Some folks THINK it is a party drug but it is also very dangerous because normally the user has no idea what the formula was to produce the drug created from other drugs. Oh yeah, ecstasy can kill you too.

GHB, also known as liquid ecstasy, is some old homemade nonsense by a do-it-yourself chemist. It has gained popularity at dance clubs and raves and is a popular alternative to ecstasy for some teens and young adults. Treat this same as you would ecstasy and avoid it by any means necessary.

Then there's heroin which is used to create the class of painkillers called narcotics - medicines like codeine and morphine. Heroin is no freaking joke and by most accounts is the worst drug out. Don't even worry about why or how people do heroin. It can kill you with ease. DON'T – EVEN – THINK – ABOUT – IT.

Methamphetamine, more commonly known as crystal meth, is a wild drug. It is very similar to crack in the sense that it is a quick and cheap high. You don't want any of this. Not only will crystal meth do all kinds of damage to you, it is crazy addictive. Users sometimes have intense delusions such as believing that there are insects crawling under their skin. Are you freaking kidding me? No freaking way. I don't want any bugs on me – real or imaginary.

LSD is a lab-brewed hallucinogen and mood-changing chemical. LSD is odorless, colorless, and tasteless. Hallucinations occur within 30 to 90 minutes of dropping acid. People say their senses are intensified and distorted - they see colors or hear sounds with other delusions such as melting walls and a loss of any sense of time. But effects are unpredictable, depending on how much LSD is taken and the user.

Once you go on an acid trip, you can't get off until the drug is finished with you - at times up to about 12 hours or even longer! Bad trips may cause panic attacks, confusion, depression, and frightening delusions.   Users often have flashbacks in which they feel some of the effects of LSD at a later time without having used the drug again.   Ummmm... I believe I'll pass and you should too!!!

Marijuana is the most widely used illegal drug in the United States, marijuana resembles green, brown, or gray dried parsley with stems or seeds.

Marijuana can affect mood and coordination. Users may experience mood swings that range from stimulated or happy to drowsy or depressed. Marijuana also elevates heart rate and blood pressure. Some people get red eyes and feel very sleepy or hungry. The drug can also make some people paranoid or cause them to hallucinate.

Marijuana is as tough on the lungs as cigarettes - steady smokers suffer coughs, wheezing, and frequent colds.

What? You didn't think I was gonna talk about cigarettes?   I'm from North Carolina!   Trust me – cigarettes are a drug.

Nicotine is a highly addictive stimulant found in tobacco. This drug is quickly absorbed into the bloodstream when smoked.   Physical effects include rapid heartbeat, increased blood pressure, shortness of breath, and a greater likelihood of colds and flu.

Nicotine users have an increased risk for lung and heart disease and stroke. Smokers also have bad breath and yellowed teeth. Chewing tobacco users may suffer from cancers of the mouth and neck. Yuck.

Nicotine is as addictive as heroin or cocaine, which makes it extremely difficult to quit. Those who start smoking before the age of 21 have the hardest time breaking the habit.

Smoking ages you.   Along with sun damage and hard living, nicotine can add years to your appearance. It may be hard, but the best thing you can do for a beautiful, glowing complexion is to stop smoking. Smoking both dehydrates and deprives your skin of oxygen, so you will see real benefits - skin will become smoother and more radiant.

Don't try and get smart and think you're fooling anyone either.   Drug addiction alters your ability to think normally.   You CAN get caught. There are such things as drug tests.   Drugs are harmful and the dependency on them can and will ruin lives.   They have powerful effects and many have not recovered from the repercussions of experimenting with drugs.   Don't do drugs because they could end up doing you, or even worse, be the end of YOU.   Drugs do kill.

As you can you see, it's a lot out there trying to rob you of your future, your youth, your beauty and your vision.   The best thing to do is to get high on life because it has much to offer a beautiful mind.

Let someone else ruin their future and their potential because you're not missing a thing...

CHAPTER 6.

Nobody wants a dumb girl...

Well of course I've got to talk about it. Education!!! A woman just ran for President of the United States (POTUS for you young ladies thinking about politics).

Yes. **Education.** I cannot stress its importance enough. I feel like Bill Cosby because you've got to know that a mind is a terrible thing to waste.

Who wants to be a dumb girl? Who wants a dumb girl? These are questions you must ask yourself when you cheat yourself out of an education.

"It costs too much." "I don't have the time." "I'm not good in school." Those are all excuses people make to keep themselves from taking the next step to success. I promise you, it's not gonna hurt you.

Be honest with yourself because please believe me when I tell you that you're not fooling anyone. The only person you are hurting is yourself by failing to pursue other avenues of knowledge. There are so many things you are capable of and there's so many things that you can do.

I'm sure some guys have no problem with you sitting on your butt all day watching TV and eating Doritos but it's not gonna get you anywhere (unless you have a crazy high metabolism and some REALLY good credit).

If you don't educate yourself in some way, can you truly bring value to a relationship? ANY relationship? Whether it is romantic, business, school, church, or organization related. Without educating yourself, you could be doomed to repeat the same mistakes over and over again.

When I say education it's not necessary that all of you enroll in Harvard or Duke. Part of your evolution as a female should be to gain life experience and schooling is but just one of them. There are traditions that must be passed on and someone must hold the torch in each generation.

There are so many avenues to pursue without college that CAN educate you. You could backpack through Europe or donate some time to humanity by joining the Peace Corps. The most important part of education is exploring and familiarizing yourself with new elements and ideas. Go and get that passport!!! You're gonna need it.

Getting out of your comfort zone is a key component of educating yourself. Too many times we are afraid to leave the nest and spread our wings. You must learn to fly before you can soar and that requires jumping off the ledge from time to time.

If you fail, then so what? Just get right back at it. Failure is a part of education.   If you learn something then there is <u>no failure</u> – only building blocks for the next time around.

So what ARE your goals?   You gotta have some.   No woman should leave home without them.   What do you want to do with your life? Do you know?

It's never too early to give some thought to some short-term goals, 3 months, 6 months, or even the next year. Have you thought about what you will be doing in five years? Where do you want to live?

Do you want to go to college and pursue a career that you find interesting? Do you want to go surfing in Hawaii or be found chilling at the Super Bowl?   Are you considering doing AIDS research in Africa or becoming an NFL Cheerleader?   It's a lot to think about.

Give some serious thought to your own goals and write them down. Plan goals for the short-term (in less than a year) and for the long-term (in the next five years). Keep these goals in mind when making important decisions.

But back to education...

Education can help you learn to think like a man. As crazy as that sounds it's also very simple. Most education is from a man's point of view. Always remember that.

It's really simple too if you can remember that "A+B=C" and that "C=D" then therefore "D=A+B". That's logical thinking in a nut shell and it's how men live. We really don't worry about if B has plans for the evening. Boys are dumb but it really is a method to the madness.

Ask questions. Now I know for many of you this will be quite natural but for some others it will be difficult. No matter what though – it's something you have to do. If they say something is clinically proven, ask "what clinic?" Cause if you don't you may find out that the hair products you are using were all approved by the Harriett Tubman Hair School for the Blind.

As far as the cost goes, there's NOTHING wrong or crazy about investing in YOU. If you'll spend $300 on a purse then you should have no problem spending a $100 on a book.

Please expand your mind. Read books. Go to a drag race. Learn to swim. Feed the homeless. Enroll in college. Take some classes. Speak with the elderly. Be the future. Be phenomenal.

Speak up! It's okay to be heard. If you feel the need then it's probably the right thing for you to do. Be aware of the world and the politics around you. Register to vote when you are old enough to do so and then exercise your right to do just that. Black people fought a long time to get the right to vote.

Also, don't be afraid to treat your job as a learning experience.   DO work.   There is nothing worse than a lazy woman.   Get up, get out, and get something.

Don't forget to network.   Network and then network some more. Networking is the art of cultivate relationships with people who can be helpful to one professionally and even personally as many times the two go hand in hand with each other. Build some relationships. Seek out some mentors. All that education, street smarts, and those good looks will only take you so far. Use all your resources because I promise you that there are many more there than you think.   You just have to look for them sometimes.

Education IS power and it can take you places you've never imagined. Just think - it made me write a book for you...

CHAPTER 7.

Do you really need those shoes?

No. I'm serious. Do you really need those shoes? I'm sure some of you have got a pair of shoes on your mind right now that you would like to buy. Nothing wrong with that – but do you NEED them?

We've got to learn to focus on Money Management and the difference between 'want' and 'need'. There's a good chance you don't need a lot of the things that you want.

For starters, start surfing the web here: http://money.cnn.com/ instead of here: myspace.com.

I'm one tragedy away from being broke so I will never consider myself "paid".

Money management can be simple but you have to be serious. It requires sacrifice and patience and if you can develop those two principles you'll be fine in the long term.

To my single mothers, I understand how kids can throw all kinds of monkeys in the system so I just pray you teach them the value of money and I'm not just talking face value and saving. I'm talking about discussing your funeral plans and insurance plans. I'm talking about taking them to the bank when you do transactions - and actually allowing them in on what's going on - if they're interested of course.

Talk to your children about current events (interest rates, mortgage failures, CEO, bailouts, etc.) and other things of this nature to help and mold a young fiscally responsible individual.

I was lucky I suppose. My mom has treated me like an adult since I was about 13. I learned how to write a check at age 8. It was a decent idea but ummm, I already liked money too much so the kid was writing checks! LOL! My mom put an immediate stop to that.

It's not about saving for a rainy day but planning for the future. This is where making short and long term goals plays into your daily lifestyle and dictates how you spend your money.

Don't focus on just getting money either. Focus on building wealth. They are two different things and something many folks don't understand.   Wealth is not necessarily measured in dollars so some things have to be acquired over time.

Value is key and it is essential to getting the most out of your money. Get the most for your money and learn to use the simple economics of 'Supply and Demand'. If they make a lot of them then there's a good chance they aren't worth a lot of money. You should try and build wealth no matter how good things are going.

But you DO have to learn how to GET MONEY.   There are so many ways to get money but the difference between building wealth are getting money are only in approach – not effort.

You can get money by baking cakes.   You can get wealth by having a bakery.   See the difference?

Taking care of your credit is very important in the past, present, and future. It is the one thing you will have to monitor as much as your money perhaps.   Your debt-to-income ratio can be a valuable number - some say as important as your credit score. It's exactly what it sounds like, the amount of debt you have as compared to your overall income.

Some simple rules for smart credit and money management include cutting down on your debt, cutting up the credit cards, don't buy it if you can't pay for it cash, watch the high interest rates, check your credit at least twice a year, pay your bills on time (just gotta say that), DO get a 401k. Get treasury bills. Get mutual funds.

PLEASE, PLEASE, PLEASE- ALWAYS get ANY agreement in WRITING.

Managing your money and your finances is essential to your growth
as individual.   It is very important to take money matters seriously.
It may sound cliché' but you really should try and save for a rainy day.
This life is unpredictable except in the fact that you can always expect
something to happen eventually.   Having the ability to be prepared
for some of life's little obstacles takes a lot of stress off of you and
makes it easier when you're looking at the new shoes in the
department store window.

Money management and financial planning are necessary not only
your future success but also your present enjoyment.   It takes
practice to get it right but you've got a lifetime worth of purchases
ahead of you.   Oh yeah – I forgot to mention, you've also got a
lifetime's worth of shoes ahead of you as well.

CHAPTER 8.

So you think you can drive?

Young ladies! Start your engines!   Some of you will be turning 16 real soon and can't wait to jump in that hot little two-seater that you just got for your birthday.

Some young females usually don't tend to love driving the way young males do.   I can remember sitting in my dad's lap trying to drive when I was only three or four years old!   The road can be stressful. But driving is a pleasure and one of your first steps toward freedom.

Driving is a huge challenge and I know it may be a lot for some of you to get used to. At the same time I know there are some young Danica Patrick's out there who just can't wait to get behind that wheel.

Seriously though, if you're at least 13 years old it's time to start thinking about driving. In many states you can still get your Driver's Permit at 15 and can also begin taking driving classes at that time.

Being a licensed driver can open up a whole new world of opportunities. But first – you gotta be ready.   There's a lot that goes into being a driver.   Think you can handle the pressure?

Learn the kind of vehicle you will be driving and get comfortable with it.   This is most important when driving a vehicle because you need all your senses when driving.

There's gonna be a lot of new roads to travel so let me be the first to tell you that there's gonna be some times when you're driving that you won't know WHERE in the world you are.   Sometimes you might just be right around the corner but lost is lost.

Never fear! In today's changing world they make navigation systems that can be placed in any car.   This does mean that you will have to learn some street names but you can now rest a little easier knowing that it has become a lot harder to get lost. I'm sure they are very helpful because I got one of my ex-girlfriends a navigation system and then she left me. Go figure.

Don't rush!!! When it comes to vehicles I know that there can be a tendency to just get in the car and drive because you have somewhere to be. You HAVE to give your vehicle a visual inspection BEFORE you get in it. This assures that you catch things that could cause damage to your tires, a flat tire, scratches or vandalism (from that crazy girl who thinks you like her boyfriend), and making sure that there is ample visibility for driving conditions.

Now when it comes to driving you need to stay focused because it only takes a split second to cause an accident. Looking down to change a radio station could mean your life. There are numerous road hazards such as animals passing through, stuff falling off trucks, crazy speeding drivers, and road construction.

Stay focused. This also means put the CELL PHONE DOWN. I know you love them to death but you've got to disconnect! Cell phones can be a huge distraction while driving.

Cell phones can cause all kinds of problems on the road. When on a cell phone you bring your conversation to the road and if you aren't having a good conversation then there's a good chance that you aren't doing any good driving as well. Your mood is very important when driving and it's best to be calm.

Also, driving with a cell phone in your hand not only decreases visibility but it also means that you have one less hand available to react to unforeseen instances in the road. Mix busy hands with a bad conversation and the day could continue to get worse.

Just in case you're in the market for your very own vehicle there's a few things we have to discuss because buying your first vehicle is very important and can set the standard for future vehicles to come.

Think you know what you want?   Well you might but regardless you should make some decisions before visiting the showroom.   Go ahead and decide what you want in a vehicle — the features, body style, pricing, etc. — before you visit the car lot, showroom, or dealership.

Stereotypical dealers will try to sell you a vehicle they want you to buy rather than what you want or need. I know you've got your heart set on a particular hot whip but it's a good idea to have two or three vehicles on your wish list, as that flexibility goes a long way toward getting the most car for your money.

Remember: The salesperson is there to make money; he's not there to be your friend. Even if yall are kin please understand that first and foremost, he's looking out for HIS money. Therefore, you should worry about YOURS.   Take your time.   Don't let anyone pressure you into buying a vehicle.

Get pre-approved by your local bank or credit union before you even start your car search.   By doing so, you'll know how much car you can buy for your money, and there's an excellent chance you'll secure a better interest rate at your personal financial institution than through the dealership's credit service which is always out to make a profit.

Do NOT let car dealerships keep running your CREDIT!   This will affect and could possibly lower your credit score. If you don't belong to a credit union, see if you qualify to join one, because they typically offer the best car loan rates.

Buying a car also builds a little vehicle equity, which goes a long way when it's time to purchase your next vehicle.

Please do consider the cost of ownership when selecting a vehicle. Find out the annual maintenance costs.   Don't forget about the cost of gas and insurance too!!   It's all kinds of incidental costs that come with vehicles so don't forget to factor them in.

If you're still in love with the vehicle the next day, then go for it!

Hooray!!! You got your car. Now what you gonna do with it? Well you gotta take care of the thing so it's important to learn a few things about car repair and maintenance. I'll be just scratching the surface here.

The key to keeping your car from turning into an unreliable clunker is to perform good preventive maintenance. If two tires are worn and two are marginal, replace all four. If the shocks are getting old, replace all four at once. If the heater and radiator hoses are old, drain the antifreeze and replace all of them at once. When a drive belt gets worn, replace all of them at once

We are on the road so much traveling near and far. Motor oil leaks, over-heating, anti-freeze leaks, transmission oil leaks, vehicle batteries, tires, and low water reserve are just a few problems that can surprise us while traveling.

Got a flat?! Oh no! It's time to talk about changing a tire! This is where all that dainty lady stuff hits that fan.

- ❖ Step 1: Choose your spot well when you pull off the road SLOWLY so that you are safely out of the flow of traffic. Try to stop in a straight part of the road, so that passing traffic can see you from a distance. Stop the car on a level spot; it is unsafe to jack up a car on an incline. Turn on your Hazard lights.
- ❖ Step 2: Remove tools from vehicle If desired, put on the gloves, and place the blocks under the tire opposite the flat.
- ❖ Step 3: Loosen the lug nuts Do not remove the lug nuts, only loosen them
- ❖ Step 4: Remove the hubcap, if necessary. Using the lugwrench, begin to loosen the lug nuts sometimes the lug nuts are quite difficult to loosen, if you can't loosen them, try jumping on the lug wrench to loosen them.
- ❖ Step 5: Jack up the vehicle by positioning the jack under the car, and raise the jack until it contacts the frame. Make sure the jack is properly positioned. Extend the jack until the tire is about 6

inches off the ground (remember: don't stop raising the car when the flat tire is just off the ground...the spare tire is fully inflated and will require more ground clearance)

❖ <u>Step 6:</u> Remove the flat tire by removing the lug nuts from the bolts, and put them aside

❖ <u>Step 7:</u> Grab the wheel and pull it straight toward you, and off the car.

❖ <u>Step 8:</u> Put on the spare tire by positioning the spare tire directly in front of the wheel well. Align the holes in the center of the spare tire with the bolts on the car. Lift the spare tire and position it on the threaded bolts. Push the tire onto the car until it cannot go any farther.   Replace the lugnuts on the bolts and tighten them, but not too tight...just enough to hold the tire in place while you lower the car

❖ <u>Step 9:</u> Lower the car with the jack until the car is again resting on all four tires

❖ <u>Step 10:</u> Tighten the lugnuts, starting with one, then moving to the one opposite it, and so on... Put the tools away and get back on the road and head to the nearest service station so that you can give the vehicle the proper attention.

You most definitely want your main method of transportation shining and smelling good so you've got to clean your vehicle.   Washing a car is a fairly easy task if care is taken to do the job properly.

Here are some suggestions for doing the best job in minimum time with maximum results:

❖ Never wash a car in direct sunlight or while the motor is still hot.

❖ Hose any excess dirt from the car exterior.

❖ If possible, using a high-pressure sprayer is best. This will help to dislodge stubborn dirt and debris.

❖ Use a soft sponge or terrycloth towel to lather the car, starting with the roof. When the roof has been cleaned, rinse the soap off completely.

❖ Repeat this process with each side of the car, including windows, tires, etc., doing one side at a time. Washing one side of the car at a time will prevent soap from drying on the car before it is completely washed.

❖ After all sides have been washed and rinsed, rinse the entire car, beginning with the roof.

❖ Using a soft dry towel, dry the car thoroughly, starting again with the roof and doing all four sides one at a time.

❖ Extra dry towels may be needed for this as towels become saturated with water.

❖ Using another towel, wipe all chrome and metal until water spots are removed.

❖ You can't forget the tire 'shine' either. It's what sets the whole wash off and makes you look like a music video star.

❖ Clean windows inside and outside with window cleaner (something I NEVER do because I hate cleaning windows).

❖ Put up all your cleaning supplies and you're ready to hit the road sparkling like a diamond.

You're looking clean and riding fly but don't forget to drive SAFE. Driving is a privilege and should be treated as such. Careless actions can leave you dead on the road.

Do not under any circumstances 'drink and drive', 'ghostride the whip', try to 'fish-tail', or 'red-line' the vehicle. If you don't know what any of that means then it's a great thing.

I've lost friends to drinking and driving so I highly encourage you to always have a designated driver if there is even the thought of alcohol being involved in your day's events. Losing friends is never fun or entertaining.

It's not all about being careless either, too many speeding tickets and you'll be waving bye-bye to that license as well (trust me on this).

Learn to remain calm behind the wheel and try to remember to drive defensively. Defensive driving will eliminate a lot of road rage. Besides, once you're late – you're late. So please don't rush like some bat out of hell. You are NOT Danica Patrick. ☺

Once you get really comfortable behind the wheel you can start thinking about accessories for your vehicle. Yep! That includes rims, mp3 players, stereos, speakers, and tint on the windows. Trust me – there will be much research required to get what fits right for you.

So you can start dreaming now, the world is right around the corner. Enjoy the ride.

CHAPTER 9.

Boys are DUMB...

I'm gonna get right to it. Boys are raised differently. We just are. We have a totally different outlook on the world from the very start of life. From a very young age boys and girls can begin to follow distinctly different paths.

Ever heard this poem?

> *"What are little boys made of?*
> *Snips and snails, and puppy-dogs' tails*
> *That's what little boys are made of.*
> *What are little girls made of?*
> *Sugar and spice, and everything nice*
> *That's what little girls are made of."*

This old school poem lets you know that the interests of boys are quite different from most females.

Just remember that with boys – EVERYTHING is about the physical. Boys don't tend to be groomed to be great thinkers. Since our youngest days most of us have had game balls and cars in our hands. That general characteristic is the EXACT opposite of how young ladies are normally raised. Young girls are taught to use their minds. They learn to play 'tea' and practice having conversations with imaginary people.

Boys, on the other hand, are out in the woods and generally taking whatever the land ahead gives them. There's a classic movie called "Stand by me" – you all should rent it because it is one of the best pictorial representations of boys just being boys. We fight each other over foolish things and then it's over. Matter solved - Problem settled.

Dealing with boys can seem very complicated and well I'm here to tell you that if you're dealing with a boy — he thinks its complicated dealing with you.

Many things can be lost in translation but it's not a matter of speaking the same language rather than being able to understand what he's saying.   When it comes to matters of the mind — or the heart, boys can be passive aggressive and in saying that 1 mean they will use actions rather than words.

Women want men to express their feelings.   What you need to pay attention to and realize, though, is that men do tell you how they feel they just do it using their own language. Men, in fact, sometimes don't use words at all when they are communicating with you.

Mostly, it's not what men say, but it's their actions that are significant. It is necessary for women to learn to interpret men's roundabout way of communicating with them.

This is where you MUST pick up the slack.   Males use sign language to convey many of their desires or dislikes.   The signs may not be the same from person to person however, so don't try and interpret an individual on the basis of other personalities.   The wrong perception could take you way off the mark.

Just remember that when you're dealing with boys they're learning how to talk to you while you are learning how to interpret them. Just don't make it too hard because the boy will usually say what he means and not mean a word past what he said.

You know what though?   You will say that boys are dumb a million times but there's one thing that you will never ever be able to deny and that's the fact that girls like boys.

Yep — that's what it is, girl like boys, and therein lies the problem. This is a dance that you will dance most of your life.   In grade school they may punch or kick you.   Somehow you're still friends with this idiot.   In middle school he may grab you from behind.   In high school, he may slap you on your behind.   It all means the same thing somehow – he probably likes you.

If he teases you about things like how clumsy you are or about how you put smiley faces in every one of your text messages. What he's really telling you when he does this is that he really likes you a lot – because he recognizes the little things.   Remember that men are just giant boys... we tease the ones we love and ignore the ones we don't.

Don't forget. Guys love the chase. Don't call him too much. By not calling him, he'll start calling you wondering what's going on.   We like intrigue due to the fact that we're all little adventurers at heart.

Once you become more comfortable with the hidden language and actions of man-speak, you'll become far more secure in your dating and relationships. So the next time you go over to your boyfriend's house and he looks at you and says, "I cleaned my room today," you'll know that he really meant to say, "I must really like you, because I can ignore my mess most of the time."

One of the best ways to learn 'male' speak, of course, is to hang with boys. This way you get to understand man-speak from a guy's point of view and a friend's perspective.

Guys do dumb stuff.   We fight. We belch.   We sing bad songs.   We can watch and/or play sports all day and never tire of it. We give each other wedgies.   I'm sure a few of you have been put in the headlock by a boy a couple of times.   We tell dirty jokes.   We just do dumb stuff and can be quite typical.

  Boys are dumb.   Get used to it.   Most of it is because we like girls.
☺

CHAPTER 10.

How to be a Lady...

Now that we've talked about the body it is now time for the mind. Is that you on that pole? You can't let society's negative images depict what makes you a woman OR what makes you valuable. Everything in life requires hard work – including integrity and dignity.

Think stripping is cool? Think it's a good way to make money? Sure, it can be both depending on where you're from but in the average guy's world – regardless of his situation – strippers are NOT considered to be the marrying type. Stay away from the pole!!!

A lady ALWAYS has a reputation to uphold.

You gotta have some sense of etiquette about yourself. What is etiquette? Etiquette is a code of behavior that influences expectations for social behavior according to contemporary conventional norms within a society, social class, or group. Etiquette is very much dependent on culture; what is excellent etiquette in one society may shock another.

In a nutshell, etiquette is all about where you are at – not where you are from. You gotta learn to adapt to all situations.

Generations ago there were strict codes of conduct that had to be followed if you wished to be considered a lady of good breeding. A lot of the stuff is easy like making sure you don't have bad breath, wiping your shoes before entering a household, and always be a gracious and good guest.

Now for some of you – being a lady is no problem, it can be second nature. At the same time, it's an image that many women hate as much as they love to represent it.

Being a lady is not easy. It's also not what you think it is – it has nothing to do with your sexuality, your financial situation, or who you know. Being a lady is a projection. It's a way of life.

This book has led me down many paths but I believe this chapter to be one of the most important in this book. It took a lot of question and answer sessions with many women from all over the globe. Of course I had no problem with that but I also found out that most of the stuff that's required to be a lady is pretty much universal.

Being a lady has no culture, no race, and no educational barriers. You can be a lady no matter your situation. There's a lot to concentrate on though. You have to learn how to dress, how to speak, when to speak, how to move, and how to react. It can be difficult for sure. However, it all starts with YOU.

Image is so important to the definition of a lady. A "lady of the night" is KNOWN to be a prostitiute. You only want to be known as a LADY. One of the first parts of this is your wardrobe.

You know they say that to achieve success you have to look the part. Whatever kind of success you are striving for you must dress for it. Contray to popular belief and whatever Lil' Kim, Trina, and Foxy Brown say – it is NOT cute to show all of your ummmm... assets!

Seriously, even though guys may give you attention for dressing 'loosely' it's not the kind of attention you want. When you are dressed in this mostly inappropriate manner all guys can see is what you put out there. That's not what you want. You want guys to fantasize a little and WONDER what could be. Trust me; you don't want to SHOW them what could be because they should be getting to KNOW what could be. Remember? Boys are dumb.

You have to learn how to be a hostess too. Welcoming people into your living space is a big part of being a woman.

Being a lady is also about turning the other cheek. You have to learn to shake off the haters and understand that feeding into their behavior will only bring all parties involved down even MORE. If those folks don't like you or how you do things then you should just move on. Trust me, it might work in math but two negatives NEVER equal a positive.

You need to know when you run into a true gentleman. It is important to learn to read a man by how he takes care of himself. It's a good identifier of how he also handles things in his life. A young man that has been trained to treat you right should not only be recognized but he should be appreciated.

I want to talk about chivalry for a hot minute. This could be a new word for some of you but the practice is far from old and should be understood not only for its merit but for what it says about you and the respect and treatment you should receive as a LADY.

There are many examples of chivalry. Some happen right in front of your eyes and you don't even realize it. For those of you with long time married parents, please pay attention to the roles that each undertakes in their marriage. I promise you that you will notice many acts of chivalry.

Old school acts of chivalry such as putting your coat down over a puddle of water (so that a woman can cross over without getting soiled) are a bit played out but acts such as opening doors, carrying umbrellas over a ladies head, and taking your hat off when greeting a lady are all acts of chivalry that are still in full effect.

There are less common examples that are to be followed however. For instance, you know you dealing with a true gentleman if he insists that you walk on his inside. That sounds a little crazy but when I say inside I mean the inside of whatever walking path you guys may be on. Basically, you are being shielded from the oncoming traffic by the gentleman you are accompanying. If you are walking on the street then the man will generally walk closest to the street and this is what I mean by walking on the inside. This also means that if we're walking in the mall – you get to walk closest to the stores and I know you like the thought of that.

In chivalry it is also common for a man to walk down the stairs/escalator in front of you and go up the stairs/escalator behind you. If you think about this it makes perfect sense because based on the man's location in these instances he is prepared to catch you should you fall. See chivalry is about much more than just being nice, it's also meant to protect women in many ways.

The newer romanticized version has recreated the woman's role, so that she is far less than weak or in distress, but still deserving of favorable treatment, specifically when it comes to who will pay for dinner. BUT – you can pay every once in a while. It's nothing wrong with that and it empowers you.

Ok, enough about chivalry. Ladies have always been considered to be fair-skinned, so what if you want tattoos!? I know you want one don't you? They're everywhere. Everyone has a tattoo nowadays. But do you really want to be like everyone? Quite honestly, if you're under the age of 18 years old you shouldn't get a tattoo for a number of reasons.

For starters, Tattoos are PAINFUL as HELL. If you don't like pain then tattoos are not for you. You will end up getting a little bit of ink and be done with the process. Then people will be asking about that new scar you have. Oh yeah, did I mention that tattoos HURT? No seriously, they do – like HELL!!!

Now I can't tell you NOT to get a tattoo because I have many of my own. I didn't get my first tattoo until I was 21 years old though. However, I've known people as young as 16 years old to have tattoos. I really think a tattoo should be well thought out and meaningful – especially your first tattoo. Your body is a temple and should you choose to scar it you ought to have a good reason why. Remember we're trying to be lady like here.

I can't tell you WHERE to get a tattoo on your body but I can tell you that I really don't want it to be visible to the entire free world. It's best to get something that can be covered up every now and then.

Remember that as a lady you will be judged on many different levels and while tattoos have grown immensely in popularity they still don't need to be shown to the world.   Remember – you are getting a tattoo for YOU.

Furthermore, I can't tell you what TYPE of tattoo to get either.   I can tell you what not to get and it's pretty much a no-brainer that you don't put some boy's name on your body.   Not a good look.

Birdies, ducks, unicorns, and such are cute when you're 19 but just think – you could be that 94 year old grandma with the faded "Southside fo' life" tattoo after having lived in North Dakota for 60 years.

But that's not all.   There's the infamous "Tramp Stamp".   Yeah – I said it.   LOL!   The "Tramp Stamp!".   I'm sorry if I offended anyone but it is what it is.   For those of you that don't know, the Tramp Stamp is a tattoo centrally located on the lower portion of your back. It's normally situated just so that if the shirt is up a few inches and a female bends over – you can see her "tramp stamp".   Seriously, this is what dudes call that tattoo!!!   Therefore, I highly recommend you use extreme thought when deciding upon the location and type of tattoo that you will be wearing for LIFE.

Life?   Wait.   Did I say life?   Yep.   But there IS an escape clause. You can have them removed!!   But there's a catch.   Remember when I said tattoos hurt?   Well getting them removed hurts THREE times as bad!   Just imagine having to remove something that has settled into your skin.   Oh yeah – they do it with a laser!!   Holy smokes!   I think I'm keeping mine.   Good thing I'm crazy.

Always try to be receptive.   Being strong minded CAN hurt you. There's a good probability that you should listen when someone tells you to do something that really only benefits you.

As a lady you should always strive to be able to walk amongst kings and queens but never lose the common touch.   You should be as comfortable at dinner with President Barack Obama as you would be with cousin Pooky. The current First Lady, Mrs. Michelle Obama, is a classic example of being able to adapt to your surroundings and hold a conversation with anyone. She is a figure to be emulated and studied.

Do keep your mouth shut sometimes. You don't have to tell anybody everything. Don't be too loud either. You can get your point across without raising your voice (believe dat!). Listen as much as you talk. You will learn a lot more by listening than you will by talking.

Be dainty. Do you know what that means? It is the essence of being a lady. It is the art of appearing to be fragile while being strong. Being dainty is the act of being delicately beautiful or charming.   It is the simple act of crossing your legs at the ankle when you have a dress on.

There is a time and place for everything so please watch how you project yourself in public (so take those rollers out before you go to the grocery store – PLEASE).

Go ahead and cry if you are hurting.   Nobody has to know. However, being dainty doesn't mean being a punk.   Take some self-defense courses if danger makes you a bit squeamish. Self-defense classes build confidence and teach valuable physical techniques a female can use to get away from an attacker or worse – a crazy ex-boyfriend.

Be confidant.   The confidence you have on the inside will show itself on the outside. As a young lady, make it your responsibility to set the tone as to how you want others to treat and respect you professionally and personally.   It will speak volumes as to how you live your life.

Always be yourself and never try to be something you're not.   People know a fake when they see one.   Be kind and considerate of others because you never know who you will see again and in what capacity.

Projecting the image of a ladylike figure is something that can take you very far in life.   Being a lady will keep them talking about you far after your life.

CHAPTER 11.

The Joy of Girlfriends...

Females talk. Men don't. Well we do talk but not about the same things as the ladies. As a man, 1 have personally had a two-hour conversation about who would win a fight between the Incredible Hulk and Juggernaut of the X-Men.

Sometimes boy-talk is just not what you're looking for. With guys, being friends is simple: 1 get mad, 1 punch you, you punch me, now we're even and we can be friends again. That's not the route 1 think most of you young ladies are trying to take however.

Therefore, you need some girlfriends!!! 1 hope you have already started making them at a young age. Solid friendships can last a lifetime and what's life without having someone to share it with?

Girlfriends give you someone to walk in the park with, borrow money from, bounce ideas off of, discuss your plans, copy homework from, STUDY with, whine about your day to, get "hook-ups" from, complain about your boyfriend with, brag about your boyfriend with, and hopefully not lose your boyfriend to.

You get mad benefits when you have friends. Girlfriends can keep you up to date. Girlfriends can keep you cool. Girlfriends can introduce you to their friends. Girlfriends can even help you get a job.

You have to learn to maintain a relationship however. You have to learn to cherish and appreciate your friends as well as put up with some of their irritating habits and/or behavior.

Some women find it harder to get along with other women than it is to get along with men. That may be because you girls can be a piece of work! A female can blow things all out of proportion and then a perception can be created that can be very hard to shake. The lying.

The gossiping. The cheating. The whispers. The secrets. The betrayals. All you have to do is add a woman's insecurity to this and it could make finding friends hard.

I gotta be straight up with you though ladies. If you want girlfriends, you have to BE the friend that you want to have. You will receive the energy that you put out there without a doubt. Don't forget that it takes work so you will get out what you put in.

It's not that hard to be a nice person. Trust me, it's something I have to work at but once you get in the groove you can smile all day. Take your girlfriends for who they are and you'll soon find out that you will enjoy them more. Be supportive and not competitive and I promise you that you could end up with too many friends.

Humility is also required in any friendship. Please ask other women what got them there, how they achieved their success, and how they balance life with their responsibilities. Sharing ideas goes a long way in the building of relationships. Learning together can give you many memories and a sounding board for your ideas.

Now you have to know how to select your friends as well. Try to pick females with similar interests and goals. This will give you much more in common and sometimes even prevent a few awkard moments. The phrase "birds of feather, flock together" didn't come from nowhere so be sure that you are in tune with your girlfriends.

Watch out for toxic/unhealthy friendships too. They are those that are unfulfilling, unrewarding and often unequal. Toxic girlfriends can stress you out, use you and wear you down physically and mentally. Don't be a crab in a barrel trying to pull others down. There is enough shine for all the girls to get their bling on. Encourage and BUILD with other women.

If your friend turns a deaf ear when you try to tell her something important to you, then you might want to ask yourself some serious questions in regards to the friendship. Friendship is a choice so be sure to get out of bad relationships so that you can move on with your life and agenda.

Don't fall for peer pressure! You can be YOU without doing anything for anyone else! Trust me, people respect a solid individual a lot more than a follower. You don't need 'em!

Watch out for "fair-weather" friends as well. These are the folks that are only around when the weather is "good." These people tend to disappear when there may be hardships in your life.

You also have to be wary of the opposite of that. That's a friend who does not pop up until things are NOT going right in their life. There's a proverb that goes "A friend in need is a friend indeed." Well of course, they NEED something from you. Make sure that it doesn't become a habit. You have to know when it's no longer friendship and you're just being used.

Life is best enjoyed with company. Your girlfriends will help you document your life over the years. They will celebrate your good times and they will feel sorrow during the bad times.

Most of all, if they are a true friend they will be there through all times. So here's to the joy of girlfriends and all the good times they may bring. Share your life!!!

CHAPTER 12.

Girl's Night Out...

It's party time! Did you pass that last test? Did you do something really well at work? Is one of your friends getting married or having a baby? Well then its time to celebrate!

One of the safest ways to go out and have some fun is with a group of your girlfriends. As a young lady it is always better to go places in groups. This way you end up in a lot less trouble because it's a lot harder to get away with something when many folks are watching.

So what's it gonna be? Where is the party at? Is it the club? The bowling alley perhaps? That new Pizza bar? Will it be the house party or the gym jam? So many places to go and as you mature there will be many more outlets for you to experience and enjoy yourself.

Well I told the boys how to get in the club for 'free' but I don't have to do that for you guys. Getting in the club is much easier for women, especially if you don't mind getting there a little early. One thing to keep in mind is that they love to let ladies in free because if there are no ladies – there's no party.

If there's an RSVP list make sure you get on it and add any one you may be bringing with you. This will insure that you not only get in but it can also keep the costs down low.

No matter where you go – you have to know your spot. Make sure you know where the ladies room is and where the exits are. Find out what the specials are and find a good spot to sit down. Atmosphere is very important when it comes to a good time and the more comfortable you are the more you will enjoy your time out of the house.

Many night spots will have dress codes but that should be no problem for you because you dressed like a lady right? Right. Ladies always get in – and many times for free.

But also, remember that danger lurks at night spots so always be aware of your surroundings. There will always be folks with bad intentions and you should always report any inappropriate actions.

One thing I can't stress enough is to **NEVER leave your drink unattended** when out on the town. Whether it be water or a mixed drink – never let it leave your sight. You don't know what someone may put in your drink that could make you sick or even incoherent.

Of course, a night out can be a wonderful time to meet someone new. Socializing is one of the spices of life so be open-minded, meet some people and be sure to have some fun.

Ok, so there's a guy in your face who just wont leave you alone and you're definitely not feeling him. You've got to get away but you don't know how. Well, let me be the first to tell you that sometimes you can't worry about hurting someone's feelings but at the same time you don't have to be a total witch to get your point across.

Learning to diss a guy is an art. If you're a lady with some skill and poise you can diss a guy and he'll leave with his dignity intact. However, some guys can't take a hint and you have to learn to dissuade them from continued pursuit.

Now you can always tell a guy that you have a boyfriend. If the guy is respectful then this is normally all you need to fend off would be suitors. But there are some unscrupulous dudes out there who lack the morals to understand what kind of commitment the word "boyfriend" truly is and will continue to press you for conversation.

At this point, what you need to do is let him know in NO uncertain terms that you are not interested and/or that you have something to do. If that doesn't work, pick up your cell phone and begin talking to someone. If he waits, go to the bathroom. Whatever you gotta do to ditch the dude — then do it and usually his attention will eventually gravitate elsewhere.

If all else fails, that's what your homegirls are for. Many of your friends will have no problem being the 'bad' girl if the guy is not interested in them so you can run for cover at the sight of the nearest friend.

Enjoy your friends! Crack jokes. Talk smack. Laugh hard. Look fly. Catch up with each other and vow to do it all again.

When the night is over always make sure you leave with people you KNOW. It also never hurts to call and inform people that you are alright once you have reached your destination. Get home safe and sound so that you may live to see the next party.

Until next time... Party on. Shibby!!!

CHAPTER 13.

Sanity is overrated...

There is a thin line between sane and insane. But you already knew that right? Ladies have no problem doing irrational things – and when I say irrational – I'm referring to a male's point of view. Most of the stuff you guys do makes perfect sense to you at the time.

Ladies, you've got to know when to draw the line! Everyone spazzes out from time to time but we don't want a few crazy moments to turn into full out insanity.

There's a movie with Martin Lawrence and Lynn Whitaker called a "Thin Line between Love and Hate" and Lynn turned into a straight psycho on homeboy and nearly killed the man. Trust me ladies – we don't want NO parts of that.

See ladies, there's a clinical 'crazy' but you guys can be CRAZY and not give a doggone about it. Most guys have to try to be crazy but no – not you. It's deep down inside and when the wrong buttons are pushed – CRAZY can happen.

There are many reasons this can happen. For starters, you ladies are dealing with a much more complex level of body chemistry than a male and that in itself is cause for concern.

Your body can easily affect your mood so it's important to monitor your body frequently. Go back and read 'Body by Supa Dave', cause knowing your body can bring an unprecedented peace of mind.

Emotions. Seriously, all I did was write the word emotions in the rough draft and then I was stumped. In a world where you can kiss a girl through the phone, a woman's emotional balance is tied to so many things. There's a reason for that and it's because you guys are just wired differently.

It's that motherly instinct. It's that natural ability to understand the importance of creating a life. It is a gift to be able to feel things deeply that can also complicate things because those very same feelings can overpower many other things. This is one of the reasons why men try to stay as far away from emotions as possible (but don't mind us, we're dumb – remember?).

Another thing that can drive you crazy is thinking too much. Because you do feel things deeply there can be a tendency sometimes to over analyze situations. STAY AWAY FROM THIS – ESPECIALLY WHEN DEALING WITH MALES. Sometimes, actually most times, a situation is what it is.

Stealing a guy's phone number? Crazy. Calling that dude FIFTEEN times in a row? Crazy. Keying someone's car? Crazy. Threatening people? Crazy. Saying you are pregnant when you aren't? Crazy. Telling a guy you love him in two weeks? Crazy. Calling someone's girlfriend? Crazy.

Sometimes you just gotta sleep on some things. Don't react. Give it a night's rest and see how you feel in the morning.

But before I get to ahead of myself, I already know that you hate that girl on Facebook and she does stuff just to get under your skin. When it comes to females, I encourage you to kill them with kindness because females don't play by the rules. Play by the rules? That would be crazy right?

Always remember. Some things are just not that serious. If you keep yourself focused on what YOU are trying to do then it wont be too much that can drive you crazy.

As I finish I know there's a few of you that can't leave that crazy guy alone. But then again, sanity is overrated right?

If that guy is crazy enough to dump you then it could leave you in a paranoid state. Moping around. Not eating. Not sleeping. Dropping pounds yo! It's something called depression and you have to be very careful with it.   Depression is very serious so learn to let things go.   Lean on your friends and don't worry about boyfriends – they'll be plenty to come and go.

Just remember to take care of yourself and learn to let it go!!   You'd be CRAZY not to...

CHAPTER 14.

Catfight!!!

Now this is something I PROMISE you that you will not see in any other book for young women. But that's the difference between me and them – I live in the real world.

You know I'm not advocating fighting but sometimes there's just no getting around it.

Remember that I told you – boys are dumb. We fight everyday. We've been fighting each other since before we knew what a fight was.

Females, however, fight for only a few reasons and that's over your man, your friend's man, or somebody else's man. Wait – it's not over a man? Then it's probably cause some female lied about you or she may simply just not like you.

Regardless of the reason – sometimes you've got to fight. It can be a matter of principle and I seriously hope you think about taking those self-defense classes I was talking about. Take Tae-bo, some Tae-Kwon-Do classes or something!

You've got to be ready at the drop of a dime because a fight is serious. A fight is also very quick and the truth of the matter is that nobody wins when females fight – except maybe the guys watching.

Wait – guys watching? Yep - that's right! You will definitely have an audience if you fight so you should really try your best not to look like a punk, wuss, sissy, or whatever they will be calling the 'loser' the next day.

You can also be smart about the situation. Sometimes it is BETTER to have an audience so someone will be around to break up the fight in case you are getting your butt whupped.

During the fight all kinds of stuff can happen. Hair gets pulled. Shirts get torn. Fingernails get broken. Make-up and hair get ruined. A fight is a few minutes of ultimate chaos — with your mind and body. JUST DON'T STOP MOVING.

Dress appropriately so that you don't end up being exposed and naked at the end of the fight. If you don't have tennis shoes on then take those heels off! You don't want a sprained ankle from having poor footing.

Anything can happen so protect that beautiful face. It's just the rules in love and war. You can apply some Vaseline to your face before the fight to help with scratches and cuts. The best way to protect your face though is to not get hit in it.

Now hopefully you'll remember to act like a lady and none of this will matter. Mature females learn to work things out. Just remember that no matter how much of a lady you are - every now and then you've got to kick a little butt.

CHAPTER 15.

How to get ANY guy...

Just like the guys, I know this is one of the first chapters you read! LOL! Trust me, we aren't that different.

The truth of the matter is that it's a different world out there when you are trying to date boys. However, you don't need to worry about boys; there are plenty of them out there. What you need to concentrate on is getting yourself involved with a young man. There's a difference between the two.

See the trick in getting boys is the same as it is for boys to get girls. You have to be a genuine person. If you pretend to be something you're not, people WILL know. But remember, boys are dumb, so even if you do like one of us – we may not know it. So how in the world does this work?

Well it starts by doing what boys do. This way you get a look into a boy's world that many other girls fail to admit exists. But if you get a chance to see what makes him tick then there's a MUCH higher probability that he will feel the same about you.

Young males are a lot less apt to try something new than a female. So you have to be smooth about introducing new things to guys. Don't be a punk but never come on too strong. Most guys really don't want someone they can walk all over so please don't behave like a doormat.

There will be guys that like certain things you like and others that don't. If you are still interested then you still may have to adjust some of your own "likes" and "dislikes".

Sports. Sports. Sports. Yes. We love them. However, that doesn't mean you should hate them. Most guys like cheerleaders because most seem like they just LOVE sports.   That's not always the case, but it looks that way – and we like that about cheerleaders.

Learn some basic things about sports, especially about the ones that the apple of your eye is interested in.   You never know, you might be a natural.   Plus, boys dig chicks that dig sports. ☺

I know some of you like to question things but PLEASE just be patient, some things will be revealed to you in time.   If it's not that serious or life threatening then let it go.   Oh, and if it's a question that has no answer – don't ask it!   Seriously, we know you do that to get on our nerves.

Appearances can be deceiving.   That's why you should really look for the guy who keeps thing pretty much the same.   At least you know what to expect for the most part from him.

You don't have to like everything about the guy but you can make subtle suggestions.   If you can accept that he might not change for YOU but he may indeed change then you will more than likely be around for a while.

Don't be clingy.   Oh – my – God.   Nothing turns a guy off more than a needy girl.   Many guys will cater to this behavior but it can play out real fast.   You want to scare a guy?   Try and force a commitment upon him, he'll be outta there sooner or later if he's not comfortable.   I promise you'll be happier if you let things develop naturally.   If things aren't meant to be, don't sweat it – it's a long life.

Do be original – makes you easier to remember.   Be natural. Be vibrant.   Be explosive.   Be caring.   We are suckers for that sort of thing.

Have something to OFFER but don't get taken advantage of.   Never let what you have to offer be why a guy wants to be with you.   Trust me, there are a lot of guys out there that will take whatever you give so you have to be careful when offering or even making things available – especially Pandora's Box.

Be humble.   The average guy wants someone to sit back and listen to him (and we really don't have a lot to say).   Don't tell him what to do, although you can always suggest – but he gets enough orders during the day most times.   The last thing he needs is another challenge to his manhood when he gets home or even when he's just chilling.   He's already carrying the weight of the day on his back so please don't add to that stress – be the answer to that stress.

There are LOTS of guys out there so don't underestimate the hardworking man.   I don't care how much money you make, your momma makes, your daddy makes, or how much you think you will make.   Just because he doesn't work in the same career field, wasn't raised the same as you, or doesn't operate like you does not mean you don't have things in common.   The same thing goes for guys outside of your race – live a little – you'll find out that we are more alike than you think.

Women in history have always dated a myriad of influences: from farmers to coal miners to factory workers.   These were honorable jobs.   These were jobs for men.   Many of those jobs no longer exist and they most definitely don't pay as much as they used to. Correction: things are MUCH more expensive.   Keep that in mind.

You can't forget about chemistry.   That's one of the first things you should consider.   Sometimes, he really is just not that into you - so don't force it. Stay away from girl haters too, nothing constructive will ever come out of a relationship with a guy who doesn't respect or cherish women.

Please do communicate with as many males as possible (not date a lot of guys) so that you can find out what you like and what interests you.   That is what I did (with females) and I did it because my momma told me too!

It REALLY helps to know what you want for yourself AND in a guy. It is important to find yourself before you can even concentrate on finding someone else.

Last but not least for sure, is to be a friend first.   Actually I'm gonna say that's the most important aspect of it all.   Young males need someone they can trust and depend upon.   Not to mention, this is exactly how you find out what a boy wants.   We are pretty straight forward in our approach.   Won't take you long to find out if he is a keeper.

Watch going backwards as well. That's why exes are always enticing - until you get around them and remember why you stopped messing with them in the first place!

Two is better than one most times and if you find a guy you like – be his friend first.   The rest will fall into place if it's meant to be.   Just please understand that a relationship is hard work.   It takes time, effort, and commitment.   Love is not a word that can be just thrown around.   You've got to fight for love.   If you're willing to do that – you can get any guy.

CHAPTER 16.

How to say NO...

One of the most difficult parts of choosing to be sexually abstinent until marriage is learning how to deal with situations where sex is all your friends and peers are talking about. Educating yourself on effective ways to let someone know "you're just not ready" is the best way to keep your future bright.

No means NO.

The choices you make today can affect your future. No one can predict if or when you'll have to confront the issue of sexual pressure. Learning how to refuse even the most common come-ons is important.

There is no right or wrong way of saying "No" to sex. As long as you make it clear that you're "not ready". If a situation feels uncomfortable or "funny" to you simply walk away and stay away.

Use body language that will get your point across clearly. Stand tall, speak clearly and be assertive. Eye contact is important when delivering your message that you are not ready.

I already told you the drugs were bad for you.   If you're drunk or high, you can't make good decisions about sex.

Don't do something you might not remember or might really regret.

Believe it or not some of the most popular come-ons have been around since your parents were teenagers. They are the lines that teens typically use to pressure or try to convince others that having sex before marriage is okay.

By knowing what some of these pressure lines are, you can develop and practice your responses before you actually encounter them.

This allows you to more confidently and firmly say "No" if you find yourself in a similar scenario with similar "smooth" talk...

- ❖ Everybody's doing it.
- ❖ Show me you love me.
- ❖ But, I LOVE you!
- ❖ Please let me share this with you.
- ❖ I'll stop whenever you say.
- ❖ If you loved me, you'd prove it by doing it with me.
- ❖ I'll break up with you if you don't have sex with me.
- ❖ Nothing will happen. I promise.
- ❖ Sex isn't a big deal.
- ❖ It's OK, I've got a condom.
- ❖ What are you waiting for?
- ❖ You mean you're still a virgin?
- ❖ I'll love you forever.
- ❖ It will strengthen our relationship.
- ❖ No one will find out about this.
- ❖ But I've done it with everyone I've ever been in a relationship with.
- ❖ If you don't have sex with me, I'll find someone who will.
- ❖ I've been tested and I'm clean.
- ❖ C'mon don't you find me attractive?

Don't let ANYONE pressure you for sex. Whatever the situation, it can place stress and strain on a relationship — you want to keep your boyfriend or girlfriend happy, but you don't want to compromise what you think is right. But forget about that – it's YOUR body!!

As with almost every other major decision in life, you need to do what is right for *you* and not anyone else. If you think sex is a good idea because a boyfriend or girlfriend wants to begin a sexual relationship, think again.

Anyone who tries to pressure you into having sex by saying, "if you truly cared, you wouldn't say no," or "if you loved me, you'd show it by having sex" isn't really looking out for you and what matters most to you. They're looking to satisfy their own feelings and urges about sex. Sometimes you could be just another notch on some random guy's belt.

If someone says, that not having sex after doing other kinds of fooling around, will cause him or her physical pain, that's also a sign that that person is thinking only of himself or herself.   And that they are just freaking crazy!!!!   Get away now. Seriously...

If you feel that you should have sex because you're afraid of losing that person, it may be a good time to end the relationship.   That person isn't worth it. Change your mind. Don't waste your time. Tell him to leave you alone.   And if that doesn't work - you can even call me and I'll beat them up for you. Just ask my sisters....   (I'm playing!) But on the real, let them get to stepping!

Say no.   To be honest, I think it's more than just a word – it's a law. Don't send false signals and don't waver. Make sure folks follow it. Seriously, no means NO.

CHAPTER 17.

Date Rape, it's not a game...

When people think of rape, they might think of a stranger jumping out of a shadowy place and sexually attacking someone. But it's not only strangers who rape. In fact, about half of all people who are raped know the person who attacked them. Girls and women are most often raped of course, but don't think that guys can't also be raped.

The large majority of friendships, acquaintances, and dates never lead to violence, of course. But, sadly, sometimes it happens. You've got to learn to watch the company you keep.

Sometimes things can go too far. When forced sex occurs between two people who already know each other, it is known as date rape.

Even if the two people know each other well, and even if they were intimate or had sex before, no one has the right to force a sexual act on another person against his or her will. This kinda stuff upsets me and it hurts me to know that so many women have endured such emotional torture.

High school boys can get out of control but date rape being inappropriate is an understatement. Punishable by law is something that should be mentioned to any overly aggressive young male – or female. Keep that cell phone near.

Although it involves forced sex, rape is not about sex or passion. Rape has nothing to do with love. Rape is an act of aggression and violence. An act of stupidity and selfishness. It is a violation of so many of a human's rights.

Remember those self-defense courses I was talking about? Don't be afraid to use that stuff! Do whatever you have to do. Bite, kick, scream, or do who knows what to protect yourself.

Unfortunately, even if someone takes every precaution, date rape can still happen. If you're raped, here are some things that you can do:

- ❖ If you're injured, go straight to the emergency room — most medical centers and hospital emergency departments have doctors and counselors who have been trained to take care of someone who has been raped.
- ❖ Call or find a friend, family member, or someone you feel safe with and tell them what happened.
- ❖ If you want to report the rape, call the police right away. Preserve all the physical evidence. Don't change clothes or wash.
- ❖ Write down as much as you can remember about the event.
- ❖ If you aren't sure what to do, call a rape crisis center. If you don't know the number, your local phone book will have hotline numbers.

Sex should be an expression of love — not something a person feels that he or she must do. Don't be afraid to stand up for your rights and report any offender. It's your body and your body is definitely not a game or something to be toyed with.

In the unfortunate circumstance that you are date raped please be sure to contact the proper authorities – don't ever try to take matters into your own hands. Seek counseling to help you get through the situation. But most importantly, remember that it's never your fault.

Life can be very serious sometimes and we must not forget that as much we aspire to seek joy. So please be cautious in your dealings with individuals.

CHAPTER 18.

911 is not a joke...

This is such a serious topic. As a black female, there is so much danger in this world. I advise you to always seek some kind of help when you feel threatened. There are different levels of threats however and how each should be handled depends entirely on the person.

I really want you to know that I would prefer that you NEVER take matters in your own hands. Not only could things go wrong and you could end up harming yourself but you could also end up with all kinds of legal entanglements. Trust me — that's not what you want.

In life sometimes you get what you ask for. We know a man shouldn't hit a woman, but don't EVER forget that a woman shouldn't hit a man either. Let's just keep our hands off of each other.

You have to be a lady. I don't advocate violence in any way. I can tell you from my own experience that violence begets violence and most times all parties end up with injuries.

Fights with anyone are not to be fooled with but fights with your spouse or boyfriend can send the BOTH of you to jail. It just doesn't make sense. So it's in your best interests sometimes if you just take yourself out of the situation.

Run! Do whatever you got to do. Just don't be involved in ANY confrontations with a man. I'm serious about this. Some of you may be tough but I would rather you save all your femininity and ego for another day. Don't get TOO hype on those self-defense classes.

Domestic abuse is NOT a game!! Domestic Violence is one of the leading causes of injury to women between the ages of 15 and 44 in the United States. Most cases go unreported.

It is estimated that every year in the United States approximately 3 million women are assaulted by their partner. One in four women in the U.S. will be assaulted by their partner over their lifetimes. Whoa. That's crazy. You might need to keep you some hot grits handy.

Domestic violence is real, according to the American Institute on Domestic Violence. 85-95% of all domestic violence victims are female. Over 500,000 women are stalked by an intimate partner each year. 5.3 million women are abused each year. 1,232 women are killed each year by an intimate partner. Women are more likely to be attacked by someone they know rather than by a stranger.

Let's talk dollars and cents. The money associated with the health-related costs of rape, physical assault, stalking, and homicide by intimate partners exceed $5.8 billion each year. Of this total, nearly $4.1 billion is for victims requiring direct medical and mental health care services.

Lost productivity and earnings due to intimate partner violence accounts for almost $1.8 billion each year. Intimate partner violence victims lose nearly 8.0 million days of paid work each year - the equivalent of more than 32,000 full-time jobs and nearly 5.6 million days of household productivity. Yo, that's losing crazy dollars kid!!

If you call the police in a heated situation, just remember that the police are nothing to play with. It is their job to arrive at the scene of a 'crime' and insure safety. They don't like false alarms too much and that could result in further complaints not being taken as seriously as they should be.

It is the LAW for the police to take SOMEONE to jail when a call is made in regards to domestic abuse. Please keep this in mind regardless of who may be at fault in this situation but most importantly – I'd rather you just remove yourself from this situation.

Don't stand for it – don't provoke it! Domestic abuse is a crime. Please, don't ever let any man OR woman hit on you or verbally abuse you. It is the kind of thing that can linger with a person if not addressed appropriately.   I want you to be a strong female and keep yourself from being intimidated.   Life is for the living.

Don't wait. Don't procrastinate.   If you are mentally abused you should take a break from things.   If you are physically abused then you should dial 911...

CHAPTER 19.

Pandora's Box...

In Greek mythology, "***Pandora's box***" is the large jar, carried by Pandora, that contained all the evils of mankind greed, vanity, slander, lying, envy, and pining—and also hope.

Pandora had been given a large jar and instructed by Zeus to keep it closed, but she had also been given the gift of curiosity, and ultimately opened it. When she opened it, all of the evils of mankind escaped from the jar, although Pandora was quick enough to close it again and keep one value inside- Hope.

Yeah, I know I'm all over the place but hey – that's exactly how I had to write this book. You ladies will keep a brother all over the place. A lot of the reason why we even let you take us through a bunch of changes is because of one simple quest and that's to take away that which should be held most precious to you.

Now I'm not trying to ruin it for the fellas – that should be your job. However, some of you are treating life like it's a field day in your pants.   I understand female empowerment and all that but since when did it become fashionable to be promiscuous?

Take it from me – not many guys are gonna turn down sex, but what do YOU get out of the deal?   You could be the girl that everyone wants to sleep with but you also become the girl that no one truly wants to be with all at the same time.

You might have a lot of new sexual feelings or thoughts. These feelings and thoughts are totally normal — it means that all of your hormones are working properly. But sometimes your curiosity or sexual feelings can make you feel like it's the right time to have sex, even though it may not be.

Though your body may have the ability to have sex and you may really want to satisfy your curiosity, it doesn't mean your mind is ready. Although some teens understand how sex can affect them emotionally, many don't — and this can lead to confusion and deeply hurt feelings later.

But at the same time, don't beat yourself up or be too hard on yourself if you do have sex and then wish you hadn't. Having sexual feelings is normal and handling them can sometimes seem difficult, even if you planned otherwise. Making mistakes is not only human, it's a major part of being a teen — and you can learn from mistakes.

Sex is no joke.   It's heavy.   Young women especially should grow into their sexuality. Sex is MAJOR.   All kinds of things are at stake.   Your freedom.   Your health. Your self-esteem. Your well-being. Your future. Your relationships.   It's something that requires you to actually THINK before acting upon.

Sex is everywhere.   Turn the TV on, open a magazine, check out your friend's most commented on 'MySpace' picture—sex sells! However, you have to keep in mind that we live in the real world, and there are consequences for not having <u>safer sex</u>.

Between 1991-2005, the U.S. birth rate for teens aged 15-19 declined 35 percent to 40.4 births per 1000 teen girls in 2005, after reaching its highest point in two decades (61.8 births per 1000 teen girls aged 15-19 in 1991). Remember that babies DO happen.

There's a possibility that one in four girls between the ages of 14 and 19 in the United States has a sexually transmitted disease (STD). That's 3.2 million girls! What's that about?! The good news is that three-quarters of teen girls don't have an STD. What about that one girl out of the four?   You don't want to be HER do you?

If you are sexually active, make sure you go to the doctor and get tested regularly for STDs.   Too many girls are only concerned about not getting pregnant.

Too many girls think oral sex isn't sex. Let me be the one to break the news to you: Oral sex IS sex. And guess what? If you're having unprotected oral sex, you can get gonorrhea, hepatitis B, herpes and syphilis.

Believe it or not, when you get an STD, oozing sores do not magically bloom on your face and your genitals don't burst into flames immediately after intercourse. Some STDs have no symptoms and many teens may not even know when they have one.

No one is invulnerable. Don't make the mistake of assuming you are. Use protection.

For women, I'm not 100% sure, but for the most part sex almost always cultivates some feelings. As a young woman there's a very good chance that you could let your guard down to someone who's not entirely worthy.

Worth. Remember that word. If you're really interested in a guy then let him prove his worth. You will know if he is putting forth the effort and if he's acting in earnest. If he's worthy then he will see the VALUE in you and treat you in a way worthy of your affection.

Now this doesn't mean to make the guys you really like wait and let the guys that you don't like have their way with you. You've got to learn to weed the bums out of your life.

MOST girls don't know their partners well enough before having sex. Sit your partner down and ask the tough questions:

> *"Have you ever had an STD? Were you treated? When did you last get tested? Are you willing to be tested regularly if we both chose to have sex? Have you practiced safer sex with your previous partners?"*

If your partner isn't willing to interrupt five precious minutes playing 'Super Smash Bros. Brawl' on Nintendo, then he or she isn't worth your time and certainly not worth getting an STD over.

Quite honestly I'd prefer you save yourself for your future husband but since I live in the real world I know that's a little hard nowadays. However I seriously advise you to take your time and make an informed decision.   There's plenty of time for all of that.

The decision about whether and when to have sex is major and it's definitely not an easy call. Should you wait for the "perfect person"? Just get it over with? Can you stop once you've started? Believe it or not, when it comes to sex, plenty more people are worrying about the same issues as you. That's why I like to call it opening Pandora's Box.

So if you have any doubts, please keep things closed...

CHAPTER 20.

Diary of a Baby Momma...

Did you open Pandora's Box?   Man I hope not but if you did then now you know some of the complexities that come with that exposure.   Motherhood is one of them.

Please don't believe nonsense either.   Many people think that if a girl has sex during her cycle, she can't get pregnant. But it *is* possible for a girl to get pregnant while she is on her cycle.   Remember that!!

Seriously, If you think birth control "ruins the mood," consider what a pregnancy test will do to it.   Always remember that sex won't make him yours, and a baby won't make him stay. And if you have sex and get pregnant, do not think that having a child will make you a wife. If he wasn't shopping for rings before you got pregnant, chances are he still won't.

Most teenagers don't plan to get pregnant, but many do. Teen pregnancies carry extra health risks to the mother and the baby. Often, teenagers don't receive timely prenatal care, and they have a higher risk for pregnancy-related high blood pressure and its complications. Risks for the baby include premature birth and a low birth weight.

Babies born in the U.S. to teenage mothers are at risk for long-term problems in many major areas of life, including school failure, poverty, and physical or mental illness.   The teenage mothers themselves are also at risk for these problems.   Some teenage girls drop out of school to have their babies and never return.

Miscarriage is also a common event in many women's lives. It is a very difficult experience. Miscarriage can leave you with many emotions to sort out.

You shouldn't play with pregnancy in any shape or form. Oh and please, please, please, don't EVER fake a pregnancy to try and "keep" a boy. Do you even know that boy's last name? Why aren't you wearing a condom?

Are you ready for all the things that a baby will bring? I know some of you think it's cute to be young and pregnant. It's not. It mostly surely isn't all fun and games. It's a lifetime commitment. No more parties. Babies cost money and time. Also, remember that most young fathers barely known their own direction.

Pregnancy, just typing the word makes me want to faint. Pregnancy can produce different emotional reactions for a young mother:

- ❖ some may not want their babies
- ❖ some may want them for idealized and unrealistic ways
- ❖ others may view the creation of a child as an achievement and not recognize the serious responsibilities
- ❖ some may keep a child to please another family member
- ❖ some may want a baby to have someone to love, but not recognize the amount of care the baby needs and do not anticipate that their adorable baby can also be the baby from hell
- ❖ some become overwhelmed by depression, guilt, anxiety, and fears about the future

Oh and you CAN go to jail for being a bad mother. If you are a single mother, you must take responsibility for making certain that your child leads a productive, healthy, and active life. You can look to mentoring programs, fraternities, sororities, church events, dance, music, arts, and athletic programs for help keeping your child active, nurtured, and informed.

If you can, it is important to keep the child's father in the child's life as much as possible. Children need their fathers. There are many intangibles to parenthood and that father can be held financially responsible in a court of law for his child should he not actively participate in or support the child's life.

However, you must remember that boys are dumb and as teenagers who have yet to mature, how much child support do you really think you are gonna get from someone who doesn't even know his own direction? That means back and forth to court and a lot of paperwork.   Do you really want those problems?

Still need more info?   Your local Planned Parenthood can help you whether you are trying to avoid pregnancy, are planning pregnancy, are already pregnant, or are dealing with an unplanned pregnancy or a pregnancy loss. You don't have to do it alone or be uninformed. Seek help and counseling if you are battling any of these issues.

Actually I told you that I would prefer if you don't have sex at all. But above all else, don't get pregnant!   You need to learn to enjoy your teenage years while getting to know yourself and your abilities. There's a lot of fun yet to be had.

Not ready to be someone's mother? It's simple: _Use protection every time or don't have sex._

CHAPTER 21.

<u>Family Matters...</u>

Seriously, it does. Family matters. If it's one thing you can hope to always count on in times of need, it's family.

A family is defined as a social unit consisting of parents and the children they raise. Hopefully, you aren't raising any kids just yet so this means you.

I know sometimes it may seem like your mom or dad has no idea what they're talking about but they really are only trying to protect you. In most cases, they've been there before and thusly know what many situations can lead to. Trust them because they are gonna need to trust YOU.

"Family values" is more than a political slogan to be pulled off the shelf at election time. Value is defined as the quality or worth of a thing. Our social values are often times reinforced by our spiritual or religious beliefs and traditions. Many people, for example, would probably agree that the values of honesty, hard work and respect for others are desirable values. But it is the values that a family develops that are traditionally the foundation for how children learn, grow and function in the world.

Defining your own family values is a combination of ideas passed down from generation to generation. It boils down to the philosophy of how you want to live your family life. Three traditional basic tasks in life have been described as work, play and love. Talk to your parents about what their focuses are. Find out what it is that they truly want from you.

And if you are a single mother just remember that the institution of slavery had a profound effect on the structure of black families. One consequence was the development of the single mother family. During the decades after slavery, single mother families continued to be formed as a result of a variety of factors, including hard economic times, husbands who died or were killed, and men and women moving from place to place in search of work. If they could do it – you can too.

Just remember that everyone lives different. What works for you and your family may not work for another's family. Some people use the church to justify family values. However, there are plenty of families who are not avid church goers. One thing is for sure, church most definitely can strengthen a family.

The American family has changed tremendously over the years though and the focus should be on living right and strengthening the family unit.

Of course, one of the best things about having family and friends is that you can all get together from time to time and enjoy each other's company.

Should it be you that's doing the hosting, remember that the host keeps the party going and make everyone comfortable. Make introductions if necessary and give out directions as need be. Show people where to sit and where the food is (you gotta have food but usually something light will suffice if it's not a holiday).

It takes a lot of patience and skills to deal with some guests so you're sure to be beat by the end of the evening. But it'll be worth it. My grandma used to do it all the time and she loved it. She set the pace for the whole family.

While I'm at it, talk to your grandmothers. There's so much knowledge and history there that you can draw upon. You can find out a lot of things about yourself and your own interests from simply asking your Grandma a few questions.

Grandma's advice can get you through some tough times even if you may have no idea what she's talking about at the time. Trust me, one day it will all click.   Even at this stage of my life I find myself doing things more and more like my grandparents did before me.

Now I'll be the first to admit that there will be some times when your family is gonna drive you absolutely crazy.   Remember that it is quite easy to forgive and forget things when it is your own blood.   Just remember that a family is a work in progress, so try not to spazz out at Thanksgiving and hurt somebody – or yourself.

Oh yeah – I'm not gonna get to into this to much but remember that when loaning money to a family member – they usually don't think it's a loan so plan accordingly.   Lots of families fall out over money! An easy rule to remember is don't loan out what you can't afford to lose.   That way you can keep a calmer head when dealing with Cousin Pooky (or you can just get him at Thanksgiving).

Just remember when you have nothing – you still have your family. Sometimes it can be a hard decision but if you try to always put your family first, good things will happen.

CHAPTER 22.

A Girl's Best Friend...

You know who a girl's best friend REALLY is right?   Of course you do!   It's the diamond!   The bling bling!   LOL!   Many girls never leave home without them.

Young ladies, I can pretty much guess that most of you have been dealing with sparkly things most of your life.   I'm sure there's nothing like a crazy glitter party even though I will have to wait on my own daughters to experience such a thing.

I've seen first hand some very interesting responses to diamonds.   I really don't know what it is that makes you girls like them so much.   However, one things for sure – I KNOW that ladies LOVE diamonds.

"Ah... some men, regardless of whether they're beasts or chivalrous knights in shining armor can sometimes sweep a woman off her feet. But diamonds – they take a woman's breath away, not sometimes, but always."   Alright, I stole that quote from a diamond ad but it really says a lot doesn't it?

When a woman wears a diamond, she wears a link to ancient history, a valuable partnership with the miners who toil night and day to come up with a diamond harvest, a "cutting-edge" relationship with expert cutters who treat their trade with reverence and an investment connection with reputable retailers.   It's more than just a rock – it's a commitment.

The name *diamond* literally means invincible or untamed.   They have been treasured as gemstones since their use as religious icons in ancient India and their usage in engraving tools also dates to early human history.

Popularity of diamonds has risen since the 19th century because of increased supply, improved cutting and polishing techniques, growth in the world economy, and innovative and successful advertising campaigns.

Diamonds. They're so beautiful. Diamond color can occur in blue, green, black, translucent white, pink, violet, orange, purple and red, though yellow and brown are by far the most common colors.

Women are fascinated and this fascination could never fade away. This is one reason why every woman, no matter what economic class she comes from, must at least have one. Even women from non-western cultures swoon over them.

But everything isn't sweet...

In some of the more politically unstable central African and west African countries, revolutionary groups have taken control of diamond mines, using proceeds from diamond sales to finance their operations. Diamonds sold through this process are known as conflict diamonds or blood diamonds.

Major diamond trading corporations continue to fund and fuel these conflicts by doing business with armed groups. In response to public concerns that their diamond purchases were contributing to war and human rights abuses in central Africa and West Africa, the United Nations, the diamond industry and diamond-trading nations introduced the Kimberley Process in 2002, which is aimed at ensuring that conflict diamonds do not become intermixed with the diamonds not controlled by such rebel groups, by providing documentation and certification of diamond exports from producing countries to ensure that the proceeds of sale are not being used to fund criminal or revolutionary activities.

So always remember to stay away from conflict diamonds. <u>The blood diamond.</u> Young people are being enslaved and are dying. This is one effort that none of us here in the States are trying to support. A wise purchase today could save a life tomorrow.

Now when it comes to a guy buying a diamond, there's a saying I've heard and it says that a man should spend at least two full paychecks on his lady's diamond ring.   That's a lot of dough but it's also part of the sacrifice you make when you have decided that you would like to be with a person.   If a guy buys you one then he most definitely thinks you are special – or he's in major trouble with you and he's saying sorry in a major way.

The most ironic reason why women crave the BLING is the fact that they are so expensive. Cost is not just the jeweler's price. It's more complex than that.   It's all about the 4 C's.   Get to know them. Diamonds are commonly judged by: carat, clarity, color, and cut .

The expense of a diamond is related to its size, the brilliance of its color, and the quality of its cut—the larger the diamond, the more brilliant the color, the better the cut, the more expensive the diamond will be. And naturally, the more beautiful it will be.

The diamond acquired its unique status as the ultimate gift of love as far back as the fifteenth century. The tradition of giving a diamond engagement ring as a promise for marriage began in 1477 with Archduke Maximillian of Austria and Mary of Burgundy.

At that time, diamonds were looked upon as talismans, or charms that could enhance the love between husband and wife. Even Cupid's arrows were said to be tipped with diamonds, which had a magic that nothing else could equal. From this time forward, the royal tradition of giving a diamond engagement ring began to be embraced by people around the world, eventually becoming as much of a milestone in one's life as the engagement itself.

All of a sudden, a woman who receives a diamond gift becomes a special and prized human being, a woman with enviable celebrity status. It's a man's way of saying, "you're quite a catch and let this diamond ring symbolize my wish that you never leave me."

But most of all, that diamond on her finger is a sign that she is loved, cherished and eternalized, because long after she's gone, the diamond she once wore will live forever.

Wearing a diamond ring on the fourth finger of the left hand dates far back to ancient Egypt, where it was believed that the vena amoris (the vein of love) ran from that finger directly to the heart. Placing a diamond, with its enduring power, on that finger, was – and still is – seen as the ultimate way to connect love with eternity.   Also, it signifies the Holy Trinity "...in the name of the Father, the Son, and the Holy Ghost."

As a representation of everlasting love, diamonds evoke the romance and magic of traditions that have spanned centuries.

The diamond is the hardest natural material known to man.   The hardness of diamonds contributes to its suitability as a gemstone. There's the saying that a diamond can cut glass and because it can only be scratched by other diamonds, it maintains its polish extremely well (but you gotta take care of it).

Unlike many other gems, you can wear it every day because the only thing that can scratch a diamond – is a diamond! However, it is important that jewelry not be stored together since it can be scratched or tangled.

Also, diamond jewelry should never be worn while doing heavy work. Points are vulnerable to chipping and even everyday activity can loosen a setting.

To be sure your diamonds always sparkle, it is important to clean them periodically.   You gotta take care of them!!! Proper maintenance will insure that you are blinging for years to come.

The engagement ring sets it off but after you get that special ring, do you know what it's time for?   That's right - it's time for the ultimate white dress...

CHAPTER 23.

White Dresses...

Remember all that talk about being a lady?   Well, eventually you get to use it.   One day you're gonna have to start wearing those sweat pants and blue jeans just a little less.

White dresses are an essential addition to a young lady's wardrobe. Young ladies if you plan on having any milestones in your life – be sure to have a white dress ready.

The white dress tradition symbolizes a seriousness of purpose and a sense of formality.   The white dress is a very significant portion of symbolism in a woman's life.   Dresses are worn for all sorts of occasions but a white dress typically signifies a very special occasion.

White dresses are worn for graduations, sorority meetings, university events, church celebrations, baptisms, Easter, white parties, building dedications, grand openings, floral events, an evening at the beach, the Kentucky Derby and just about any function during the summertime.

There's nothing like a good "white" party to make you feel not only fly but also a part of a whole.   White parties tend to have very casual atmospheres and encourage socialization.   Usually a recipe for good times.

I wanted to get more information so I hollered at some of the wonderful ladies of Spelman College.   They directed me to the Spelman College Reunion website.   I found some very interesting information too.

The ladies at Spelman College are encouraged to buy white dresses before even stepping on campus and have been doing it ever since the early 1900s.

According to Spelman College at www.spelman.edu, the traditional white dress attire is as follows:

- ❖ A solid white dress or a skirt suit. The dress or suit should be "true" white -- not off-white or cream.
- ❖ Flesh-toned hosiery
- ❖ Black, closed-toe shoes
- ❖ Functional jewelry only, which consists of a wrist watch and rings worn on the hand

Seeing as how the ladies of Spelman have always been upstanding women, I'm gonna take their word on white dress attire. You should too.

Then of course there's the ultimate white dress. Hmmmm... What could that be?

The wedding dress! The wedding dress is traditionally white as a symbol for purity but the wedding dress can be any color. The white wedding dress is merely a formality now but the intent is there.

A couple hundred years ago getting married in a white dress was all about wealth. Getting married in a white, extravagant gown was a sign that you could afford to buy a dress that you would never be able to wear again because of its style and color (whites were not as easy to clean in those days as they are today! Well, except by me, I can't keep a darn thing white).

White is deemed the most fitting hue, whatever may be the material. It is an emblem of the purity and innocence of girlhood, and her new commitment to the chosen one.

Choosing a wedding dress? Well, I'll leave that up to you. ☺

And if you're not the bride, there's a good chance you could be in a few weddings in which your dress really doesn't matter. Seriously, I've never EVER heard of a female liking her bridesmaid dress. It's a fact of life – deal with it.

There's an even higher probability you'll be attending a wedding sometime in the near future, probably at least once a year for many of you for the rest of your life. There will be a lot of weddings ESPECIALLY after you go to college (which of course, I'm encouraging you to do).

As you get older, you may feel the need to take someone to a wedding with you. If you do this, don't take just any guy – especially not to make yourself look attached. Dudes are already very wary of weddings because all they do is make people think of marriage. Crazy hunh?

But seriously, don't take just anyone because you will get comments like, "So when are you two getting hitched?", or "We'll start planning your wedding next." See that's just madness. Make sure you enjoy your wedding date. Make sure your date is the type that can enjoy a wedding as well.

Go solo and enjoy yourself if you have to. Just remember to have fun and help the bride celebrate her big day.

Besides, I'm sure you've got your eyes on a white dress of your own...

CHAPTER 24.

Parting Words...

To all of the young ladies reading this, if you don't know anything else, I want you to know that you are filled with potential and life has so much in store for you.   But I must remind you that it is a long journey and that you must remain focused.   Patience and wisdom will be necessary and you should work on these traits accordingly.

Throughout life there will be many naysayers, pitfalls, accidents, misunderstandings, and all other kinds of stuff that will try and derail you and your plans.   Stay away from the negativity and regardless of what happens, I promise you the sun will still rise another day.   You may not see it but it's shining somewhere right above your head.

Don't ever let anyone try to knock you down. You are the future and therefore you must be steadfast.   Your self-esteem should not be rooted in anything but you.   Don't worry about the things that you can't control.   Use that energy for all the things that you can.

Take pride in the things you do well and continue to improve them. If you nurture your talents you won't have time to let anyone knock you down.   If someone is bringing that negative energy your way just look the other way.   Tell them to keep it moving. Scram. Skee-daddle...   Don't even underestimate the power of positive thinking.

Confidence is a tough thing to build but if you believe in yourself then you will have no choice but to get stronger with time.   A focused mind is hard to take for granted. Always strive to do the best you can with what you have and I know for a fact that the rest will fall into place.   It doesn't matter if you fail, lose, or get sidetracked, always remember to learn from your experiences and move on.

Need some examples of confidant women?   They are all over the place.   Oprah is the bomb but Madame C.J. Walker was the first black woman millionaire.   Mary J. Blige bared her soul and after facing her demons she came out a smooth pearl after life's perils. Afeni Shakur has used the deaths of many friends and family members, including her son Tupac Shakur, to continue to affect the lives of young people. Wilma Rudolph was an Olympic athlete that battled the disease Polio as a youth before she became an Olympic legend.

So please stop feeding into the magazines. Stop comparing yourselves to the girls in the video. God only made one of you. Even if you've got a twin – it's still only one of you. There is no perfect girl. There can only be a perfect you and that comes from believing and being confidant in yourself.

It's not easy for some. Confidence is something that must be practiced. I'm so good at it some might even call me cocky. But you're a young lady – so don't be like me. Be better than me.

Don't mistake being strong-minded or difficult for confidence either. If someone tells YOU to do something for YOU – then you should really think about what that person is saying to you. Especially if the only person that will benefit immediately would be YOU.

I implore you to focus on your strengths while building up your weaknesses. Be honest with yourself too. If it's something you know you need to be working on then do that. Don't make an excuse to neglect yourself. Make time for yourself. Learn to understand your VALUE. Treat yourself. LOVE yourself. Remember that this is all about love.

Nobody is gonna take care of you like you so pamper and spoil yourself. Love yourself like no one else can. No matter what it is that you do, you should know that you are someone of value. I know you're the bomb so hopefully now you always will too.

I've already taken up to much of your time; it's time to get to work. I'm out! Peace! Until next time, God bless and live strong,

CHAPTER 25.

Special Shout outs...

Now for the fun part, you know how we do baby! Got to give love to my people! I am so unbelievably blessed to have a talent I can share with the people. It is with the support of my friends and family that I'm allowed to express myself without thought of repercussion.

I thank God and my lovely Mother, Dr. Jenny Perry-Horton for all their strength and guidance.

"Mama – there's no way I could pay ya back but my plan is to show you that I understand." Tupac Shakur

I'd like to give a very special thank you to Ms. Afeni Shakur for allowing the usage of Tupac's verse and all the folks at the Tupac Amaru Shakur Center for their support. It has meant a lot to me. Special shout out to Maxi and Yzette and her company, onedestinypublishing.com. Now can I get on the invite list?

A very special thank you goes out to the Burwell Family for providing my beautiful cover girls, Ms. Jayla Burwell and Ms. Kennedy Burwell.

Wow, so many people supported the last book – my family, my friends, my colleagues, my classmates, the community, the police (lol!), and the church. The support has humbled and encouraged me in ways you guys wouldn't believe – and if you know me then that's one heavy statement.

To my support group, all of my love goes out to Robert and Autumn Alston, The Chambers Family, The Kiel Family; The Cash Family, The Burwells, The Butterfields, The Parkers, The Hines Family, The Graham Family, and of course, the Horton and Perry Clans.

To my inspirations: Ms. Nikki Giovanni, Ms. Maya Angelou, Mr. Carter G. Woodson, and Ernest Hemingway. Thank you for allowing me to understand that nothing is more important than education and motivation.

Yall know life is incomplete without friends and I've made a lot along the way in this crazy life of mine. Whether they be near, far, new or old – you are appreciated and I thank you for adding value to my life.

I would be nothing without the kids! Special thanks to all the kids at Meadowcreek High School in Metro Atlanta; J.T. Williams Middle School in Charlotte, NC; Morrow Middle School in Metro Atlanta, and all the young people whose path I've crossed. You guys have been the greatest and have filled my life with wonderful memories.

I'd like to thank the whole state of North Carolina! I love calling North Carolina home.

To my Alma Maters: North Carolina A&T State University and Georgia Tech – thanks for all your guidance, mentoring, and support. Duke Law School – here I come...

Special thanks to my brothers in The Sons of Durham. Your tireless efforts to spread love make the City of Durham, NC a brighter place.

To Ms. Terri Baskin for helping me with all of my website needs. You have been a wonderful addition to the team.

Thanks to my man big dog Gil Robertson. Thanks for allowing me to participate in your work. It's a Family Affair!

All my love goes out to the members of the Bloody Mu Psi Chapter of Omega Psi Phi Fraternity and all the bruzz in general. Roo to the Ques! F.I.E.T.T.S.

Special shout out to the World's Busiest Airport: Hartsfield-Jackson Atlanta Airport, and all of my co-workers.

My humblest thanks to the lovely ladies that offered their advice:

- ❖ Ms. Sahar Simmons
- ❖ Ms. Nesha Harrell
- ❖ Ms. Ky'leigh Wilson
- ❖ Mrs. Jenelle Lyons
- ❖ Ms. Kelly Mayfield
- ❖ Ms. Tomeka Hall
- ❖ Ms. Bridgette Herring
- ❖ Dr. Tysianna Jones
- ❖ Attorney Endi Piper
- ❖ Ms. Twyler Crawford
- ❖ Ms. Crystal "C.J." Simpson

This book wouldn't have been the same without your input and thank you for your time and friendship.

Shout outs to all the cool folk I've met along the way – thanks for chopping it up with a brother:

De La Soul, Talib Kweli, Dougie Fresh, Lil' Webbie, Bishop Eddie Long, Donnie McClurkin, Goodie Mob, DJ Nabs, Carl McNair, Sandra Wimberly, Helen Blocker-Adams, Sherri Scott-Novoa, Nikki Turner, Hill Harper, Omar Tyree, Morris Chestnut, Larry Corn (roo dog!), Andre Rison, Elton Brand, Flava Flav, Theo Ratliff, James Cotton, TakeoverTV, Malik Yoba (I'll never forget the kind words brother), J. Anthony Brown, Afrika @102 Jamz, Screenwriter Previn Taylor, Comedian Garrick Dixon, Cushcity.com, The Duke Basketball Report, Art Franklin, and Professor Griff.

My photographer: Damon Thomas. I appreciate you my man. Yall can hit him up at www.expressivecapture.com.

My legal eagles: Ms. Endi Piper, Ms. Pili Fleming, Ms. Jade Fuller, Mr. Jay Greene, Mr. Bryan Smith, and Mr. Brenton Boyce, Jr. (don't test me!!!)

Rest in Peace and you will not be forgotten to Chris Chavis, Hugh Hunter, Latonya Williams, Fred Harris, Karen Matthews, my father David Horton, my grandfathers, my Aunt Julia Mae McCoy, and my beloved grandmother – Ms. Gladys Perry.

Thank you for all your love. I promise to continue. I won't stop – cause I can't stop.

Dang, and I'm still growing...

Oh and call me what you want, just don't call me late for dinner...

Supa!

"Live all you can; it's a mistake not to. It doesn't so much matter what you do in particular, so long as you have your life. If you haven't had that what have you?"
-Henry James

Notes: